The Wiccan Guide to Self-Care

The Wiccan Guide to Self-Care

A witch's approach to healing yourself

MARIE BRUCE

This edition published in 2023 by Arcturus Publishing Limited
26/27 Bickels Yard, 151–153 Bermondsey Street,
London SE1 3HA

AD010585UK

Printed in the UK

MIX
Paper | Supporting
responsible forestry
FSC
www.fsc.org   FSC® C171272

CONTENTS

INTRODUCTION
CHECKING IN...

In this book of psychotherapy-based witchery and self-help, you will learn practical ways to improve your life, your general wellbeing and your overall mental health. Life fluctuates and we all experience ups and downs, highs and lows, so it should come as no surprise that mental health fluctuates accordingly. There may be times when you feel that you are at rock bottom and can't take any more. Conversely, there may also be times when you are so happy it hardly feels real. Be aware that some of the happiest life events, such as getting married, getting a promotion at work, or having a baby, can often be very stressful indeed, so you might find yourself wondering why you are not enjoying these things as much as you could, or imagined that you would.

At such times in life, it is useful to have a tried-and-tested set of tools you can use in order to ease the stress, to identify and neutralise your emotional triggers, and generally regain control of your head space. That is where this book comes in. As a qualified psychotherapist, I have clinical experience in helping people to weather the storms of their lives, enabling them to come to terms with whatever circumstances they find themselves in. From helping the bereaved, as a Cruse Bereavement Care counsellor, to assisting military personnel to cope with Post Traumatic Stress Disorder (PTSD) and battle trauma, I have a range of experience and a variety of wellbeing tools that I have successfully used in the therapy room, and in daily life, that I have drawn upon in writing this book.

As a practicing witch I also believe in the power of spirituality to improve mental health and wellbeing, because having faith that life is a blessing goes a long way towards making it so! This guide is aimed at readers who just want to read a book that can help them to feel better *right now*. It is written in an accessible style, keeping the psychotherapy lingo to a minimum, explaining complex things in real terms, without oversimplifying them. In addition, I have included lots of charms, spells, exercises and mediations to keep the magic flowing through your life, even during the darkest of times, which is when you need it the most.

Essentially it is a Battle Plan for life. So no matter what challenges or issues you face, the psychotherapy strategies and magical techniques within these pages can support you, helping you to navigate a safe and positive path forwards. These are tools used by counsellors in therapy rooms across the world and they are highly effective.

I will show you how you can reduce anxiety, calm stress, identify people and situations that are bad for your mental health, recognise your personal stressors and triggers, soothe feelings of being overwhelmed, increase capability and take charge of your mind, rather than letting your mental state control you. This book will show you how to take back control of your life. So if you want to free yourself from a negative past and look to the future without fear and anxiety clouding your judgement, you're in the right place!

You can work through the chapters at your own pace. All you need is a commitment to change and the courage to put the strategies I present here into regular practice, plus a notebook to track your thoughts, reflections and progress. So without further ado, let's begin your personal journey of magical self-help, as you begin a practice which leads to a healthier head space and a happier life!

Serene blessings,

Marie Bruce x

CHAPTER 1

THE WISE WOMAN

A long time ago, before the arrival of modern medicine, the wise woman was one of the most important and respected figures in any town or village. Her responsibilities were many and varied. They included things like mixing up herbal brews and birth control remedies, working as a midwife and a shepherd of souls, laying out the dead. She would also act as a confidante, offering advice and wise counsel to those who sought her help. She knew everyone in the village, including all their family secrets, which made her a powerful figure.

The old country term for a witch was *wise woman* and the two terms are often used interchangeably. The wise woman played a vital role in local society, as she helped the crops to grow and the livestock to thrive, using her spells and charms for good weather and to ward away illness. She was frequently called upon to act as midwife to both women and animals. She would also be sent for when someone was dying, bringing sleeping potions and pain relief, to make their passing easier.

More than this, the wise woman was something of a local agony aunt. People would go to her for advice and guidance, comfort and a listening ear, but she was no push-over. If she thought someone was whinging, she would give them a good dose of tough love and send them away to rethink their attitude!

A WISE WOMAN'S WELCOME

In a sense, being a counsellor and psychotherapist is exactly like being the wise woman of old. We offer the truth, even when it stings a bit: we highlight where people are self-sabotaging or bringing their problems upon themselves. At the same time, we offer comfort and a listening ear to those in genuine need, helping them to get back on their feet after a setback of some kind, be this divorce, bereavement, redundancy or whatever else.

So what could you expect if you came into my witch's therapy room in need of help? First of all, you'd get a warm welcome and you might pick up on a soothing, calming atmosphere. This is because I bring gentle magic to my clinical practice, not to proselytise – my clients have no idea that there is magic in the room, they just feel calmer as a result of it – but to protect the space, the client and myself. Being a counsellor is a tough job. You spend a lot of time listening to tales of horrendous trauma, accidents, deaths, abuse and so on. It is the darkest side of life staring you in the face and you see it over and over again, one client after another, day after day. It can bring you down if you let it, so of course I try to protect myself from the negativity as much as possible.

I also like to protect the space in which I work, whether I am seeing clients one to one or simply sat in my study writing about psychotherapy in the hopes of helping people whom I will probably never meet, so I always cast a circle before I get started. I want my work to be light, bright and happy. I want my words to reach out as a beacon of hope to my readers and clients, so that they know it's okay to struggle: it doesn't make you weak. Acknowledging the struggle and working through it is what makes you stronger. I want the room in which I see clients to feel welcoming and to have that 'sparkle' that positive magic always leaves behind – you can't see it, but people can feel it and it comforts them.

I make sure that I open the windows and invite the spirits of air to bring in the winds of change, which is what my clients need. I light a candle to show that we are working in the light of a higher force, whether you call it the Goddess, Spirit, God or the Universe, something bigger than me is guiding the session. Many counsellors work with card decks – the Blob deck being most popular as it helps clients to get in touch with, and express, their emotions. They also use pebbles and stones to represent family members or future goals. I do all of this, but I add in a sprinkling of magic as I go, so I am just as likely to use a deck of angel oracle cards as the Blob cards. Angel cards are particularly useful when working with the bereaved and they quickly release lots of emotion. I use crystals too – I always ask a client to pick out a crystal to take away with them on our last session. Amethyst and rose quartz seem to be the most popular, but snowy quartz goes fast too. Ordinary beach pebbles can be used as worry stones for anxious clients, or wishing stones for those who are ready to start planning for their future again.

I protect myself by imagining that I am surrounded by a pink bubble that is filled with pure white swan feathers – the room and my client is protected by the cast circle, but this bubble protects me from the negative vibes they inadvertently bring in with their troubles, while the swan feathers cushion the blow of hearing bad things and reminds me that there is more purity in the world than darkness. It's a simple visualisation exercise but it works. And what kind of wise woman would I be if I didn't offer my clients a soothing witch's brew? As I make their tea or coffee I silently call on the healing, cleansing powers of water to help my client to feel better and at the end of their session I say: "Take care of yourself. Bright blessings until next time." In this way I am sending them away with a blessing that is non-denominational.

When the psychotherapy session is over, be it writing or counselling clients in person, I like to play a bit of music to eradicate any leftover negative energies, as I take down the circle and clear things away. I thank the four elements of earth, air, fire and water for their aid and I go about my day, happy in the knowledge that I have helped someone, just by listening and being there for them. As you can see, being a witch and a psychotherapist go together like black cats and pointy hats! It's all just part of being a Wise Woman.

So welcome to this, our therapeutic space upon the page! Here, you are safe to share and let go of whatever you need to. Here we are going to work magic together, to improve your life and your overall wellbeing, one step at a time. Self-care is one of the greatest acts of kindness you can offer yourself. It is a set of tools that keep you healthy, happy, motivated and achieving. It isn't something that you do once and consider it done. It is a daily practice that becomes a habit, and the habit becomes a more positive lifestyle.

PERFORMATIVE VS. TRANSFORMATIVE SELF-CARE

No matter where you are in your life right now, whether you are at rock bottom, or just feeling the need to pamper yourself a bit more, self-care is a powerful tool, yet there is far more to it than simply running a bath! When most people think of self-care, they imagine lighting a candle or having a massage, yet this is really only surface level self-care. Many self-care books stick to this surface level of information – have a shower, use a body scrub, put on a face mask etc.

There is no doubt that such simple tasks can help you to feel better in the moment and they all have their place in self-care practice, but they are the *performative* aspects of self-care. In this book, however, we are going to go much deeper, getting right down to the root of the problem and working with transformative aspects of self-care too. Let's take a look at the differences between these two types of self-care.

PERFORMATIVE SELF-CARE

Performative self-care is the quick fix. It usually pertains to the body and to your external self. It is the simple things that you can do to make yourself feel marginally better *immediately*. It's the long soak in a hot bath after a hard day at work, the brisk walk in the fresh air, the soft glow of a candle burning, the squeaky clean feeling of freshly washed hair. Performative self-care holds a key place in any self-care practice, and it is often the gateway through which people begin to explore deeper levels of self-care, such as counselling or therapy.

Performative self-care is great for an immediate boost to your mood, or for building up several simple tasks into a solid routine. Because let's face it, there are times in life when a simple task is all that you can manage. Maybe you have been recently bereaved, or you suffer from depression or a chronic illness. At such times, going deeper might feel like too much, so this surface level of self-care is extremely valuable during such difficult times. But performative self-care only goes so far and it rarely leads to a lasting, positive change. For that, you need *transformative self-care*.

TRANSFORMATIVE SELF-CARE

What do we mean by *transformative* self-care? Well, if performative self-care pertains to the body and your external self, then *transformative* self-care is all about your internal landscape – your mind, your emotions, your spirit and spirituality, your past, your beliefs and so on. Transformative self-care is about excavating your inner self, developing greater self-awareness, addressing your past, identifying triggers, building your resilience and so on.

Transformative self-care uses tools such as journalling, free-play, free-association, mindfulness, meditation, visualisation and so on. It is focused on how you feel and what you think. It is a way of checking in on yourself each day, so that you can be more in tune with your emotions, thereby developing your emotional intelligence. It is transformative care that takes place in the therapy room and which leads to lasting, positive change. Transformative self-care is the long-term solution.

HOW TO USE THIS BOOK

Transformative self-care takes work. It takes time, but sometimes a quick fix is really all you need and all that you're looking for. With that in mind, I have designed this book to include both levels of self-care. Each chapter will include tips, tricks and tools for both surface and deeper level practices. If you are looking for a quick fix, you will find them under the *Simple Self-Care* heading, while deeper, more transformative techniques can be found under the *Deeper Healing* heading. Ideally, you should use both levels of care whenever you can to achieve the best results, but if all you can manage right now is the surface level, then go with that. What is most important is that you begin. Just make a start on looking after yourself and do whatever feels right for you at this moment in time. You can always come back to the *Deeper Healing* tools at a later date. In addition, there are more traditional magical practices here too, so if you are looking for spells and rituals, you will find these under the *Witchy Ways* heading.

I also suggest that you have a notebook handy. This should be something that you keep just for your self-care practices. In this book we will be using journalling, mind-mapping, time-structuring, free association and so on, which are all techniques that benefit from being written down. You can open a new computer file if you don't like to write by hand. Alternatively, you can use a voice recording device. If you *can* use a journal, then I strongly recommend that you do so, as there is a form of magic in transferring your innermost thoughts onto the page, when writing by hand. Use a fairly large one to give yourself room to work. If you are cramping your entries onto a tiny page, you are stifling your personal growth, so allow yourself space to think freely on the page.

In addition, create a safe space for yourself in which to read and work through the practices of this book. Look back at how I prepared the therapy room for my clients at the start of this chapter and see what you can do to similarly prepare your own space. Can you lock the door so you are not disturbed, or turn off your phone? Can you open a window to let fresh air circulate, or grab a calming drink, such as camomile tea? Do whatever you can to let your mind and spirit know that your self-care is sacred time. Looking after yourself is a serious business, but have fun with it too. Wear fuzzy socks with a silly motif that makes you smile, or write your journal in multi coloured inks. Just do what you can with whatever you have.

MIND ALCHEMY

Witches know that the most powerful tool they possess is their mind. Many of the tools in this book might not, at first glance, seem to be that witchy at all, but that doesn't diminish their power. Appearances can be deceptive. Often, the most effective spells are cast with very few magical tools. This book might not be full of witchy bells and whistles, but the clinical techniques within these pages are designed to create deep and lasting positive change – and that transformation has to begin in the mind. It is a kind of metamorphosis. It is the alchemy of the mind, turning darkness and shadows into light, and that is pure witchery!

TAKE IT EASY

I want this book to become a trusted tool of support for you. Self-support is the best kind because you are the only person who is guaranteed to always be there when you need help. Having said that, sometimes we all need a little bit of extra guidance, and I hope that this book will provide that guidance for you. You don't have to read it from beginning to end if you don't want to. You can flip through to the topics and tools you feel you need the most right now. In this way, you can begin your journey of self-care immediately. And it is a journey. This is not something that can be achieved overnight, for we are working towards emotional intelligence, mental resilience, general wellbeing, letting go of the past, overcoming obstacles and creating a life that serves you better. Such things take time, so go easy on yourself. There will be days when you can't face doing any of the tasks or spells in this book, and that's okay. Tomorrow is a new day. Push yourself, but don't force yourself.

Do I have to be a witch to use this book?

In a word, no. It is more important that you maintain an open mind and a willingness to do the work necessary to make positive changes in your life and to your routine. Self-care and deep healing are for everyone, and so is the natural magic of the universe. You do not need to identify as a witch or Wiccan in order to benefit from the tools and techniques in this book. Everyone is welcome here.

SELF-CARE IS A PRACTICE

Self-care is a practice and practice makes perfect! The more time you give to your self-care the more proficient you will become at it and the better you will feel. At first you might only feel better for short periods, say while you are doing a *Simple Self Care* task, before sliding back into your old emotional rut. That's okay. Back-slides are normal and it is all part of the process. However, as you build your practice into a daily routine, maybe adding in the odd **Deeper Healing** technique too, you will begin to notice that you start to feel better for longer. You may even start to look forward to your self-care practices and the routines that you have built and created for yourself. Don't be afraid to adjust and adapt your routines so that they fit more easily into your day. If you have more time during the day when the kids are in school schedule in your self-care, then, when you have the house to yourself. Likewise, if you work all week, just do the surface level self-care on work days and leave the deeper healing techniques for the weekends when you have more free time. Tailor the practice of self-care to your own needs.

CHAPTER 2
SKILLS FOR MODERN SELF-CARE

S elf-care is a natural part of a witch's daily routine. A magical life is one that supports your hopes, dreams, ambitions and wellbeing. As witches, we know the value of quiet time alone with our thoughts, we understand the importance of releasing the past and the skills required to restore balance in the body. We make herbal tea to ease a headache and add essential oils to the bath water to sooth aching limbs after a hard day. We mix up massage potions and home remedies, lending a touch of enchantment to our healing ways.

Perhaps even more importantly, we know that we cannot be effective magically if our body and mind aren't in good shape. Stress means that our spells simply won't fly! It is essential therefore, that we look after ourselves in mind, body and spirit, if the magic we want to cast is going to work. Self-care is simply a mindful extension of enchanted living, because magic and self-care are complimentary practices, leading to an empowered and happy life.

THE BENEFITS OF SELF-CARE

There are many benefits to developing a good self-care routine, not least of which is that you will become more attuned to the natural rhythms of your body. This in turn means that you are more likely to notice when something is out of sync, or not as it should be, enabling you to work some healing magic, or seek medical attention, sooner rather than later. For some illnesses, such as cancer, this early intervention can significantly improve chances of survival. Even for more minor ailments, the sooner you notice them and take healing action, the less likely they are to become any worse.

The same is true for your mental health too. In journalling and working through the deep healing exercises in this book, you are more likely to understand where your habits and behaviours come from, what issues might still be holding you back and if you need more professional help, such as one to one counselling. While the teachings of this book are rooted in the powerful psychotherapy practices I have successfully used with my clients, it is no substitute for personal counselling, so if something is flagged up as you read, please reach out and seek professional help. There is a list of useful phone numbers and websites in the Resources section at the end of this book, and don't forget that your GP is often a great first port of call, as they can signpost and refer you on to specific help available in your own area.

PAMPERED PRINCESS

Pampered, spoilt, overindulged, over-privileged, cosseted, entitled… these are just some of the words hurled at people who enjoy the good things in life and who are not afraid to show it. These negative associations towards taking care of one's own needs are rife within society. They can have a deep impact on your personal view of self-care, and in turn, on how well you look after yourself.

There is no doubt that some people experience a deep sense of guilt when they do anything that is just for them, including self-care practices. They might believe that they are wasting time, being lazy or narcissistic. If you can relate to this, then please bear in mind that there is nothing wrong with addressing your own needs and ensuring that they are met. In fact, it is one of the perks of being an adult! Children require an adult to provide for them and meet their needs, you don't. You can, and should, provide for yourself as much as possible, especially when it comes to something as personal as self-care, because one size doesn't fit all. Your self-care practice should be tailored to fit your personal issues and needs.

There is also the assumption that self-care denotes laziness and is non-productive, when in fact, nothing could be further from the truth. Self-care takes time and energy to perform properly. It is deep work, drilling down into your psyche to find out what's really going on, producing results of positive, lasting change. Remember that you are worthy of your own time and that pampering is not a dirty word!

ENCHANTED INDULGENCE

Wiccan self-care is about lending a sense of magic to your pampering and self-excavation work. It is a form of enchanted indulgence, where you focus solely on yourself for a time. It incorporates spells, rituals, meditation, visualization, affirmation, journalling, and so on. It can help you to develop your magical skills, while you figure out where you are and what you want from life. It should not be regarded as frivolous and it doesn't mean that you are spoiled. It simple means that you love and respect yourself enough to give time and attention to yourself, on a regular basis. Prioritizing yourself in this way means that, to a certain extent, you can become self-healing, as you address issues from your past and create new positive habits of behaviour that support you much better, going forward.

WITCHY WAYS: COMMIT TO SELF-CARE
In this little ritual you are going to make a magical commitment to your own self-care. Take a pink or white candle and anoint it with rose or lavender essential oil. As you rub the oil onto the wax with your fingers, make the decision that are going to commit a certain amount of time each day or week to self-care practices, be this journalling each day or by making the Survival level of tasks in the next chapter, non-negotiable. Once you have decided how

much time you want to commit and when, set the candle in a holder, light the wick and say the following incantation to seal the ritual in magic.

Time for me, time to be free, even when time is rare

Digging deep, every day, I commit to my own self-care

Day by day, each step I take lifts my spirits higher

I love myself, I respect myself, this commitment is forged in fire.

PRACTICE PRETTINESS AND THE ART OF BEAUTY

Humans are visual creatures and so our moods are heavily influenced by our surroundings. Think back to the last time you saw something beautiful and how it made you feel. It might have been the sight of the sun setting over the ocean, a towering forest of pine trees or your sleeping child or pet. This uplifted sense of happiness is how your home should make you feel too. There is a lot to be said for the art of living a life filled with beauty. Again it is one of those things which society often berates you for, telling you that you are spoilt if you want to fill your home with beautiful things, but beauty is an intrinsic aspect of happiness.

We all know someone who seems to have everything – a great job that they love, a happy family, loving relationship, money in the bank, a nice car, exciting holidays, their own business, the perfect pet and so on. How does it make you feel to think of such an individual? Are you inspired by them and motivated to work on achieving your own goals, or do you feel envious and belittle their success as a result? Do you consider that person to be spoilt, over-entitled or undeserving of their success? If so, try not to be so hasty in your judgment, because chances are that they have their own issues to deal with too. No-one is perfect. No-one's life is perfect either, even though it might seem that way at times.

Having said that, there is one thing that such seemingly perfect people *do* tend to get right and that is the art living a beautiful life. They tend to practice prettiness on a daily basis. By this I mean that they make a conscious effort to bring pretty things of beauty into their life regularly. When they need to make a new purchase for the home, they are mindful of its aesthetic contribution to their surroundings. Given time, this mindful approach to nesting builds into a stunning home, filled with prettiness, which can appear to denote a perfect life, and while none of us can ever achieve perfection, we can all be more mindful of the things we surround ourselves with and their effect on our mood.

SIMPLE SELF-CARE: PRACTICE PRETTINESS
Take a good look around your home right now. Does it spark a feeling of joy, comfort, safety? Is it well tended, clean and tidy? As you look around, can you see things that are beautiful to you, which lift your spirits and make you smile? Take a few moments and see how you can improve the prettiness of your surroundings right now. What can you do to bring beauty in? Could you go and buy some fresh flowers or a new house plant, do a quick speed clean, organize something, frame some photographs, play a bit of music? Think of one or two small tasks that you can do today to begin practicing prettiness in your home and see if this raises your mood.

SMALL JOYS AND LITTLE WINS

Self-care is a journey to becoming healed and whole, one which should leave you feeling a little stronger, a little happier, the more you practice it. It doesn't happen overnight though. It is a process. That said, although you might not shake off a deep depression after just one magical bath, it is important to celebrate the small joys and little wins along the way.

Daily happiness is made up of small joys – the laughter of your child or lover, the birds singing, the feel of the wind in your hair, especially after rounds of chemotherapy or temporary alopecia! Each tiny moment of joy can add up to a day of happy smiles and that is worth acknowledging and celebrating, because it acts as confirmation that good things are always happening.

Little wins are important too – getting home before the rain pours, cleaning out the clutter drawer, finishing work early, receiving a free gift of some kind, an unexpected compliment, reverse parking the car without a mishap, ticking off a task from your to-do list and so on. Little wins like these often go unnoticed, but if you acknowledge them as they happen, it increases your motivation to achieve more and enhances your sense of personal capability.

Both of these techniques are especially important the closer you are to rock bottom. When you are feeling very low, simply getting out of bed and having a shower is a little win and you should acknowledge it as such. Celebrating the small moments of joy and the little victories is a form of gratitude. It confirms that, no matter how bad you feel, the world turns, the birds sing, life goes on and you are still capable of victory and joy every day.

SIMPLE SELF-CARE: KEEP A TALLY
Start to keep a tally of all the small moments of joy and the mini victories that you notice throughout the course of the day. The more you count them, the more you will notice and soon you will be listing a myriad of things to be grateful for. *Enjoy* your life. You

are not immortal and it doesn't last forever. Learn to appreciate the here and now.

SELF-CARE ON A BUDGET

There is no doubt that self-care is often presented as something expensive and luxe, involving trips to a spa, professional beauty treatments, luxury creams and lotions. This could be one of the things that discourages people from the practice, because they feel that they can't afford it. It can be very disheartening when you pick up a book or a magazine for tips on better self-care, only to be presented with a shopping list full of items you might not want, or are unable to afford. The same can be said of witchcraft, where expensive, specialist tools are often regarded as being essential for spells and rituals. They're not.

In truth, you can practice both witchcraft and self-care with the items that you already own. You don't *have* to go out and buy expensive products. In a pinch you can use regular table salt in a bath potion, rather than a pricier pink Himalayan variety. Herbs can be gathered from the gardens of friends and family members and dried at home, or picked up quite cheaply from most supermarkets. Plain white candles can be substituted for candles of any other colour. Crystals and essential oils can be interchanged and substituted for the ones you already have, providing they are in alignment with the purpose of the spell.

The main tools you will use for magical self-care is your mind and a heart that is open to personal excavation and growth, so if all you have is a note pad and a pen, you can still experience the many benefits of a self-care practice simply by working your way through the *Deeper Healing* techniques in this book. That said, many people enjoy practicing magic with candles, crystals, oils and so on, and therefore, I have included the tables of correspondences below and tips on how to use particular items as self-care tools. Please bear in mind that this is not a shopping list, and you don't need to purchase all these items. It is just useful information to have to hand if you need to substitute one crystal or herb for another.

MAGICAL CORRESPONDENCES

Any tool that is used in spell craft is called a correspondence. There are correspondences for all different types of magic and you will need to know what these are when you come to start writing your own spells. Below is a list of Magical Correspondences for the most popular types of magic, so that if you don't have what a spell calls for, you can look at the Correspondences and switch to something else that has the same associations. This should work just as well and it will stand you in good stead when you come to write your own self-care rituals. Of course, if you have had great success with a particular herb or crystal, then keep using it, but in general, these are the Correspondences that work well for these types of magic.

MAGICAL CORRESPONDENCES FOR LOVE AND SELF-CARE

Colours: Red, pink, lilac, white, light blue

Crystals: Carnelian, rose quartz, ruby, diamond, clear quartz, citrine

Herbs: Rose, rosemary, peony, lavender, lilac, elder flower, myrtle, ivy

Oils: Rose, geranium, ylang ylang, lavender, neroli, frankincense

Incense: Rose, strawberry, ylang ylang, night queen, sandalwood

MAGICAL CORRESPONDENCES FOR PROSPERITY AND SUCCESS

Colours: Green, gold, silver, white

Crystals: Aventurine, jade, iron pyrite, clear quartz,

Herbs: Basil, bay, cinnamon, tea leaves, sage, mint, sunflower

Oils: Patchouli, frankincense, sunflower, rape seed

Incense: Cinnamon, frankincense, night queen, patchouli, dragon's blood

MAGICAL CORRESPONDENCES FOR PROTECTION AND RESILIENCE

Colours: Black, grey, dark blue, purple, dark red, white

Crystals: Hematite, onyx, amethyst, sodalite, smoky quartz, labradorite

Herbs: Thistle, rosemary, basil, holly, turmeric, garlic, mugwort, foxglove

Oils: Tea tree, bergamot, eucalyptus, cedar wood, pine

Incense: Pine, sage, night queen, patchouli, dragon's blood, black pepper

MAGICAL CORRESPONDENCES FOR PERSONAL POWER

Colours: Black, purple, red, white, your favourite colour

Crystals: Hematite, amethyst, clear quartz, smoky quartz, snowy quartz

Herbs: Lavender, rosemary, basil, sage, mugwort

Oils: Tea tree, patchouli, eucalyptus, pine

Incense: Pine, sage, night queen, patchouli, dragon's blood

THE SPARKLING BENEFIT OF CRYSTALS

Self-care is often about cleansing, rebalancing and bringing the light back into your life. Crystals are one of the quickest and easiest ways to achieve this. There are hundreds of different kinds of crystals, but some of the most useful include snowy quartz, clear quartz, blue lace agate, iron pyrite, snowflake obsidian, black obsidian, sodalite, carnelian, citrine, amethyst and the much loved rose quartz.

Having crystals dotted around your space means that when the sunshine hits them, they will sparkle, glimmer and glow. Their energies will gently infuse the space, making it feel more positive. They are an easy way to practice prettiness, with the additional benefit that this type of crystal magic attracts all good things - love, wealth, positivity and so on.

There is a purity to crystals and crystal magic that lots of people are drawn to. They help to make a space feel light and free of negativity, especially if you have amethyst, as it soaks up any negative energy and neutralizes it. All crystals can help to create a pure space, which is especially good if you have been down in the dumps for a while. Any lingering negative vibes are instantly cleansed away, just by the presence of the crystals. That's the beauty of crystal magic - it's relatively effortless, so it is perfect for when you are in a low-energy state. Providing you cleanse the crystals regularly, they will keep attracting the good and neutralizing the bad. Below is a list of some common crystals and what they represent in self-care magic.

Amethyst: calming, soothing, neutralising, absorbs negative energy

Black Obsidian: fore-shadowing, despair, grief, loss, torment, contraction

Blue lace agate: healing, soothing, tranquillity, flowing movement, visions

Carnelian: wounds, deep emotions, overwhelm, trust

Citrine: communication, energy, joy, happiness, sociability, opportunity

Clear Quartz: clarity, objectivity, purity, amplification

Green Aventurine: growth, anti-fatigue, energy, expansion, stability

Iron Pyrites: abundance, prosperity, finances, savings, security, cash flow

Rose Quartz: love, acceptance, gentleness, positivity, radiance, beauty

Smoky Quartz: banishing, depression, anxiety, uncertainty, stagnation

Snowy Quartz: innocence, purity, coldness, isolation, rigidity, frozen heart

USING CRYSTALS IN SELF-CARE

There are many ways in which you can incorporate crystal magic into your self-care rituals. You can use any size crystal, large or small. Polished tumble-stones are usually the least expensive, but you can also find much larger crystals if you prefer a more visual cue, though these can be quite expensive. Some of the rituals in this book include the use of crystals and the smaller stones are quite adequate for the magic presented here. You might already be an avid fan of crystal magic, enjoying the power of these sparkly gems, or you may never have used them before. Either way, here are a few examples of how you might draw upon their power for self-care.

- *Sleep with a crystal tucked into your pillowcase*

- *Hang one or two water-safe crystals in a pouch from the bath tap to let the water run over them as you draw your bath*

- *Use crystals to draw out your magic circle, placing them on the floor all around you*

- *Use four crystals to mark out the cardinal points of your home or space*

- *Place a crystal on your third eye, in the middle of your forehead, lay back and meditate. See what comes up.*

- *Lay down and place the appropriately coloured crystals along your chakras and mediate.*

- *Hold a calming crystal in your hands when you feel anxious or overwhelmed.*

- *Wear power bead bracelets or items of jewellery with crystals in them*

- *Scatter them around your home to fill your space with vibrant, positive natural energy.*

THE SOOTHING BENEFITS OF ESSENTIAL OILS

Essential oils are another easily accessible form of magical energy work and aromatherapy has been proven to have a beneficial impact on those who use it regularly, lowering stress levels, calming anxiety, aiding restful sleep and so on. Most large chemists sell essential oils and you can use them in several different ways. Add a few drops to the bath water, or to your pillowcase, simmer them in water with a diffuser, sprinkle a few drops onto a tissue or handkerchief and breath in the benefits, or mix them with a carrier oil, such as almond oil, to create your own massage potions. You do not need a huge selection, but lavender, tea-tree, ylang ylang, lemon balm and peppermint are all goods ones to begin with as they can each be used for a variety of purposes and issues.

PICK A CARD, ANY CARD!

Tarot and oracle card decks have been a favourite tool of witches for hundreds of years. These days there are so many interesting decks to choose from, so you are bound to find one you like. Learning how to read a spread of cards will offer insightful information to you about yourself, the world and your place in it. Most witches tend to pick a single card from their preferred deck each day, to see what the energies of that day are and how they might make the most of it. Again, this is a very simple form of daily enchantment that you might like to add to your self-care routine. Both my Moon Magic and Celtic Magic oracle decks have been written with beginners in mind, but you can just as easily use a deck that you already own.

SIMPLE SELF-CARE: AURA CLEANSING RITUAL

Your aura is the energy field which protects you spiritually. It is made up of colours – the lighter and brighter the better. A dark aura is indicative of illness, addiction or the accumulation of bad energy. Although some people can see auras, for most people it is not noticeable. It is something that magical practitioners often visualise as a glow that surrounds the entire body. If your aura is bright and healthy, you will feel happy and energetic. If it is dull and contaminated with dark energy however, you will feel sluggish, tired and lethargic. It is therefore a good idea to get into the habit of cleansing the aura with a simple visualisation exercise.

Stand or sit in a comfortable position and visualise your aura all around you. Raise your arms high until your palms meet over your head, then slowly lower your arms, imagining that you are pushing any dark colours down and into the ground where they will be neutralised by the earth. When your arms are by your side, breathe deeply three times, then slowly raise your arms up again, this time imagining that you are pulling light, bright colours into your aura from the earth. When your palms meet, your aura has been cleansed. Try to do this at least once or twice a week, or incorporate it into any stretching or exercise routine you do, as part of your cool down process. This will help to ensure that your aura doesn't become too clogged up.

Now that you have seen how easy self-care can be, are you ready to begin? Let's start with what to do when you're at rock bottom...

CHAPTER 3

ROCK BOTTOM

Rock bottom is a horrible place to be. While the good news is, the only way is up, the bad news is, it is still one heck of a climb! When you are at rock bottom you feel like you are *existing*, rather than actually *living* your life. Simple tasks become much harder, small setbacks seem like insurmountable obstacles. Your brain has moved into survival mode and you don't have the mental bandwidth for anything beyond the basics.

There are many reasons why someone might find themselves at rock bottom and it has nothing to do with weakness. Usually it is as a result of a major life shift. Events such as bereavement, a devastating diagnosis, a life changing injury, divorce, an accident, losing your job, becoming a victim or witness of a serious crime, old battle traumas and so on, can all send someone plummeting straight to rock bottom. This is normal. It's not nice, but it is normal.

Rock bottom and the depression that usually accompanies it, isn't necessarily a bad thing. It acts like a time-out, meaning that it gives your mind the space it needs to process what just happened. This is why your mind goes into survival mode, because you need to free up bandwidth to come to terms with the change in your circumstances and to work through the emotions the change has brought about. Your mind cannot do that unless it goes into survival mode, at least for a time.

The real problem occurs when someone has been at rock bottom for a long period of time, when it becomes their everyday life and their uncomfortable comfort zone. Even a dark place can become a comfort zone if you let it, because it becomes familiar to you.

It becomes what you are used to. This is when people often turn to harmful coping mechanisms. When someone is at rock bottom, they are more likely to self-medicate, using drugs, alcohol, food, shopping etc., to make themselves feel better in the short term, but in the long term, they are just stacking up more problems, because not only do they still need to process the original event, now they might have addiction and debt issues to contend with too, or at least, an unhealthy pattern of behaviour to correct. But what does rock bottom actually look like and how do you identify it? Below are some of the classic warning signs that someone has hit their lowest point.

WHAT ROCK BOTTOM LOOKS AND FEELS LIKE

- *Consistent low mood and/or depression*

- *A feeling of hopelessness – like nothing will ever change*

- *A feeling of helplessness – you just don't know what to do*

- *Lethargy – everything seems like too much effort*

- *Paranoia – it feels like life is out to get you*

- *Low immunity – you pick up every bug and virus that's going around*

- *Unexplained aches and pains – your body feels too burdensome to move*

- *Insomnia or sleeping too much – you might switch back and forth, between the two*

- *Indecisiveness – you can't make a simple decision*

- *Apathy – you just don't care about anything anymore*

- *Anxiety – your thoughts spiral to darker and darker places*

- *Head spinning – your mind keeps racing*

- *Floating head – you are not in tune with your body*

- *Disconnection and dissociation – feeling separate from yourself, others and the world around you*

- *Overwhelmed - you feel like you just can't cope*

- *Doom scrolling – you seek confirmation that the world really is horrid!*

- *Lack of appetite/ eating too much – again you might switch between the two*

- *Self-medicating – drugs, food, alcohol and so on*

- *Self-harming behaviours – cutting, burning, scalding etc.*

- *Poor hygiene and self-neglect*

- *Unkempt house*

- *Stagnation – you just feel stuck*

- *Suicidal thoughts/plans*

- *Attracting toxic people*

These are all signs that you have reached a very low point, mentally, emotionally and physically. How long you have been in this phase will determine how much of an impact it has had on you and your life. Sometimes, one event leads to another. The initial incident sends someone to rock bottom, but being in such a low state for a prolonged period can trigger other events to occur, such as a relationship break down, homelessness or a job loss. This compounds the misery of the initial event, leaving the individual with even more to cope with, but there is a way through to the other side and this book can help you to get there. The following magical exercise will give you the space and protection you need to begin processing your thoughts and feelings.

WITCHY WAYS: CREATE YOUR BUBBLE OF PROTECTION
Rock bottom is when you are at your most vulnerable so it makes sense to put a touch of protection magic in place before we go any further on your self-care journey. This is a simple visualisation exercise, one that you can do anywhere. Imagine that you are surrounded by some kind of bubble, similar to the one I described in Chapter 1 when I was preparing to see clients. This bubble is your circle of protection. It keeps all the bad vibes away from you and guards your space from external negativity. You can visualise your bubble in any way you like. It could be made of thorny plants, water, snow or something else. Close your eyes, visualising yourself within the centre of the bubble and say:

The bubble of magic is all around me, none can do me harm

The bubble keeps all ill at bay, while all within is calm

SELF-NEGLECT AND SELF-ABANDONMENT

When someone is at their lowest ebb, often the first indication, is that of self-neglect. They stop taking care of themselves. They stop making an effort with their appearance. Their home becomes untidy, cluttered and unkempt. They stop getting their hair done. They might not shower or brush their teeth. They don't cook nutritious meals, but rely on junk food to sustain them. This goes back to what we looked at earlier, about people being in survival mode. They will do the bare minimum in terms of personal hygiene and caring for their home.

This doesn't mean that they are being lazy, or dirty or that they don't care how they look anymore. Often, they feel embarrassed by their appearance, they might even apologise for it, but they don't have the energy to do much about it. We call this self-neglect and it is the direct opposite of self-care. It is a clear indication that something isn't right. If you see someone who is looking a little rough around the edges, it is likely that they are going through something you are unaware of, so show them some compassion. Likewise, if you can relate to any of this, show yourself the same level of compassion you would give to a friend. We all have odd days where we neglect to wash our hair, or fail to keep on top of the housework, but if this becomes a regular pattern in your life it means that you are in a state of *self-neglect*, possibly even self-abandonment.

Although both terms are often used interchangeably, there is a subtle difference between the two. *Self-neglect* is when you fail to maintain even basic levels of hygiene, appearance and feeding yourself properly. Imagine a neglected child and what they might lack, for instance, they might lack food, drink, fun bath times, play time and toys, warm clothes, waterproof shoes and so on. When you are in a state of self-neglect, the only thing you are providing for yourself is that same *lack* of all the basics.

Self-abandonment however, is when you abandon your own needs, wishes, desires, goals and so on, in order to fit in with someone else. When you put someone else's desires first, at the expense of your own, or when you sabotage your goals, then you are in a state of self-abandonment. Mothers do this all the time, as they constantly self-abandon in favour of putting the needs of their children and family first. Fortunately, self-care is a great antidote to both scenarios, so let's take a look at the different levels of self-care and what they represent.

SELF-CARE LEVEL 1: SURVIVAL

This is the base line, the minimum standard of care that you should be giving to yourself every day. When you are at rock bottom, the tasks in this level might be the only ones that you can manage, and they could well leave you feeling exhausted afterwards. Nevertheless, the items on this list will help to keep your life ticking over and will prevent you from falling too deeply into self-abandonment or sabotaging behaviours that store up future problems, such as forgetting to pay your bills!

Survival Self-Care Skills

- *Showering or bathing*

- *Brushing hair and teeth*

- *Getting dressed*

- *Eating nutritious food*

- *Buying groceries – have them delivered if you can't face the supermarket*

- *Get some fresh air, even if only through a window*

- *Pay your bills on time – automate them using direct debit or standing order. This takes one thing off your plate and means you don't have to worry about missing a payment or falling into arrears.*

- *Check in with yourself – how are you feeling right now. Give yourself a score from 1 – 10, with 1 being rock bottom and 10 being on top of the world. Write the score in your journal or on a calendar. Notice how your mood fluctuates from day to day and week to week.*

- *Talk to a loved one every day, even if it's a pet or a house plant!*

- *Create a routine – more on this later.*

SELF-CARE LEVEL 2: AWAKENING

This level of care is for when you are starting to pick yourself back up again. However, if you want, you can also incorporate one or two of these tasks into your daily routine when you're at rock bottom, alongside the survival care skills. Pick the ones that feel easy. Don't take on too much at once.

The Awakening phase is when you are just starting to feel a little bit better. I refer to it as an awakening, because you are starting to look around you and notice things more. This is when you realise that you haven't watered the plants for a while, or that the laundry has built up while you've been feeling down in the dumps. The Awakening phase of self-care is delicate. It cannot be rushed. Remember that you are still fragile. Whatever happened to send you crashing down to rock bottom is still your reality, and that knowledge might hit you all over again from time to time. You might oscillate between feeling okay and feeling wretched.

Again this is perfectly normal and all part of the healing process. The care skills at this level are a mixture of simple self-help and deep healing tasks. Bear in mind that this is not a to-do list. Rather it is a series of things you might do to support your Awakening and keep moving forward. Just pick out two or three to complete each day and see how you get on.

AWAKENING SELF-CARE SKILLS

Simple Self Care Tasks

- *Try to go outside for 20-30 minutes – tend your garden or just sit in the fresh air*

- *Gentle exercise for 20-30 minutes, i.e. walking, dancing or stretching*

- *Art therapy – draw out your mood or your emotions, try colouring in, painting, pottery, crafting etc.*

- *Meditate*

- *Visualisation – imagine a better future for yourself*

- *Use affirmations – see Chapter 3*

- *Take a 20-minute power nap*

- *Give yourself a facial*

- *Listen to soothing music, make a playlist*

- *Use a face mask*

- *Give yourself a manicure*

Deeper Healing Self Care Tasks

- *Journalling*

- *Mind Mapping*

- *Emotion tracking – keep a track of your moods and triggers*

- *Time Structuring – plan out your day*

- *Take up a rainy-day indoor hobby you enjoyed as a child*

- *Spend time in nature*

- *Invite a friend round for a chat – let them come to you at this stage*

- *Making plans – what do you feel like doing today?*

- *Declutter and organise a small space*

- *Do small household tasks such as laundry*

- *Sort through post and paper work and shred anything you don't need*

SELF-CARE LEVEL 3: EMERGING

This is when you begin to emerge from your self-imposed hibernation. At this stage, you start to feel a bit claustrophobic because you have been cooped up for too long. You crave fresh air and sunshine, and like a butterfly emerging from its chrysalis, you are ready to stretch your wings and see more of the world. It can feel quite scary, particularly if you have had a long period of time away from society, as you came to terms with a loss of some kind.

Remember that this stage of your self-care is a form of recuperation, so don't take on too much at once. Allow yourself extra time to complete tasks, as you are likely to feel exhausted quite quickly and things will take longer than usual. This is a good time to get on with all those little things that might have been bugging you during your rock bottom phase. Enlist the help of a friend or family member to help give your space a facelift with a lick of paint, or have a good decluttering session. This will act as a sign to yourself that you are ready to make a fresh start and you are moving into a new phase of your life. The tasks at this level are all deeper healing exercises, designed to get you moving forward and thinking ahead.

Emerging Self-Care Skills

- *Deep clean your home – do one room a day to keep it manageable*

- *Paint a room*

- *Declutter*

- *Organise your kitchen cupboards*

- *Organise your wardrobe and dressing table drawers*

- *Sort through makeup and toiletries, discarding anything past its best. Do the same with medicines.*

- *Take a trip to a charity shop to donate your unwanted items*

- *Go to a friend's house for a visit, or go on a nice outing together*

- *Make a dream board*

- *Create a list of goals you would like to achieve*

- *Book a holiday or theatre tickets to give yourself something to look forward to*

- *Adopt a pet – but make sure it is one you can manage and afford, even if it's just a goldfish.*

- *Go to a salon and get your hair styled professionally*

- *Buy a new crystal that you feel attuned with*

- *Buy new house plants or work in your garden*

- *Sort through your witchy supplies and replenish them as needed*

- *Take up a new hobby or a class that gets you out and about*

- *Go for a drive, a ride, a skate or a swim*

- *Walk in the woods or through a park*

- *Take up gentle exercise as part of your weekly routine*

- *Practice mindfulness*

SELF-CARE AND RECOVERY FLUCTUATES

Bear in mind that self-care and deep mental healing is not a linear process and you will inevitably slide back and forth between the three levels of Survival, Awakening and Emerging. Things might be going well as you Emerge out into the world again, but a small set back, some bad news or simply doing too much too soon, can all send you straight back to Survival level. This should not be viewed as a failure. It is simply how the process works. Just make sure that you keep doing the self-care tasks at the appropriate level for your mood, and in this way you will still be moving forwards and making progress. It might not always feel that way, but even small incremental steps will get you somewhere.

NO MAN IS AN ISLAND

Human beings are social creatures. We need the company of others in order to thrive, maybe not all day, every day, but every now and then we need to interact with another person. Even introverts start to crave human contact after long periods of solitude. However, when you feel down in the dumps, socializing is often something you avoid. It feels like too much to take on. You don't want to have to put on a brave face and so its simpler to refuse invitations and just stay home. After a while, the invitations might stop coming and this in turn can lead to irrational feelings of rejection!

It can feel quite intimidating to start socializing again when you have been at rock bottom for a while. You might wonder how people will react to you, if your friends still have time for you, or how they will address any change in your circumstances, such as the loss of a partner or a job. But you *do* need company, so the trick is to gently dip your toe in the water and see how you go.

If you used to go out in a group, meeting pals in the pub each week for quiz night, for example, a good tip is to call your most understanding friend first, a few days in advance, so that they can lay the groundwork with other members of the group. Explain that you are ready to socialize, but you might only come out for an hour or so. Also, ensure that you flag up to your friend any topics of conversation you wish to avoid. This means that everyone knows where you stand and you can begin to socialize again on your own terms.

This works with family members too, especially those who have been a bit distant. Some people avoid those individuals who are going through a tough time because they are scared of saying the wrong thing. Let friends and family know that any *foot-in-mouth* situations will be forgiven. It might even be just the thing to break the ice!

Above all, please remember that no matter how bad you are feeling, your presence in the world acts as a comfort to someone else. Who is that person? Give them a call and make plans to meet up.

SIMPLE SELF-CARE: AUTOMATE EVERYTHING!

Being at rock bottom frequently means that simple everyday tasks get neglected or forgotten about, so make this time easier on yourself by automating as much as possible. Spend an hour or so automating all your household bills, setting up standing orders or direct debits, so that they are paid automatically. In addition, create an online master shopping list with your chosen supermarket, so that you can simply add to it week by week, without having to start from scratch. This means that you can have all the basics and essentials delivered in the click of a mouse. It might seem small, but taking these simple everyday tasks off your plate will free up time for you to work on other aspects of your self-care and healing journey, while at the same time ensuring that all your bills are paid on time and there is always food in the cupboards. Easy!

DEEPER HEALING: DRAW A MIND MAP

Mind-mapping, or clustering, is a technique used by psychotherapists to help a client actually see what is going on in their mind. It quickly highlights everything that they are dealing with, what they are holding on to and trying to process. It can be quite an upsetting exercise, but it also acts as a form of validation for their feelings. A typical response to drawing a mind-map for the first time is something along the lines of *"Well, no wonder I feel so bad with all this going round in my head!"*

Try this exercise when you are in a safe space, preferably when there is a trusted loved one within calling distance, as this task can be quite distressing. Mind-mapping is like lancing an abscess and squeezing out the puss. It can be painful, but it has to be done for the healing process to begin. You know what they say – better out than in!

Take a large sheet of paper and in the middle write a keyword that sums up what you are going through. Examples could be Bereavement, Illness, Redundancy, Battle Trauma (or the country where the trauma occurred i.e. Afghanistan or the Falklands) Abuse, Divorce etc. Write your keyword in the centre of the page. This is the root cause. Next, write down all the words that you associate with the root, including any events which came about as a direct result, such as loss of a limb, relationship breakdown, financial insecurity, divorce etc.

Keep going until the paper is as full as you can make it. Try to cluster related items together. This usually happens naturally as you think of them in sequence, but you can draw lines and circles to link up words and events on the mind-map. This isn't an artistic exercise. It's not meant to be pretty. Most finished mind-maps are a mess of criss-crossing lines, words grouped in bubbles and the keyword in the middle, with everything else spanning out from that central point and root cause.

Just write it all down as quickly as possible. See what comes up. Let it flow. Remember to include words that describe how you feel as well as the events themselves. You will know when you are finished because you will feel a sense of relief and exhaustion at having extracted all the darkest aspects of your life in one sitting! This is by no means an easy task. Once you have your completed mind-map, sit back and take a good look at it. Everything on that sheet of paper is what you have been carrying with you, in your heart and mind, possibly for years. Is it really surprising that you've been feeling a bit down in the dumps? Probably not.

Mind-mapping can bring out many emotions and reactions, from anger to sorrow, tears to tantrums, pacing to prattling, but it is a useful first step in self-care because until you can see what is going on for you, you cannot begin to address it. You might know that you have been feeling stressed, without being able to pinpoint where that stress is coming from. A mind map helps to pinpoint it. Keep your mind-map safe, as you will be referring back to it during the course of this book. Finally, if this exercise has left you feeling particularly agitated, perform a couple of the Simple Self-Care tasks from the level 1 list to regain your equilibrium.

CHAPTER 4

SELF-SABOTAGE

People can often be their own worst enemies, creating lifestyles and habits which at best add to their stress, and at worse can be downright harmful. If you are too hard on yourself, showing yourself little to no kindness or compassion, then you are likely to feel a deep sense of unworthiness. Likewise, if you are a perfectionist, you might be inadvertently adding to your personal stress levels by trying to do everything perfectly, all the time, which simply isn't possible. If you are self-medicating with drugs or alcohol, as a way of coping, then this is a form of self-harm.

It is also true however, that most people don't even know when they are self-sabotaging and cannot identify their own sabotaging patterns of behaviour, which means that they cannot interrupt the pattern! In this chapter we are going to explore what it means to self-sabotage, why people do it and what habits you can create to minimize your self-sabotaging patterns.

IDENTIFY YOUR NEGATIVE PATTERNS

Self-sabotage is the adopting of negative patterns of behaviour. For instance, if you want to save money to buy a house, but you are consistently over-spending and dipping into your savings for frivolous things you don't need, this spending is a form of self-sabotage, because it is a negative habit which keeps you from achieving your goal. Another example is that of someone who is severely stressed by their workplace, but who refuses to take time off sick or look for another post, thereby keeping themselves stuck in their current stressful role. Inaction can be the subtlest form of self-sabotage to identify, yet it is also incredibly effective at ensuring your failure to thrive.

It goes back to the self-abandonment we discussed in Chapter 2, where you might put the needs of others before your own. Self-sabotage means that although you are acknowledging your needs, your behaviour does not support them, but holds you back instead. In essence, all negative patterns are a form of self-sabotage so it is vital that you recognise your own negative patterns of behaviour and begin to build better habits to replace them.

Self-sabotage is a consistent, day to day, failure to thrive. While everyone has some self-sabotaging tendencies, learning to identify what yours are, can be the difference between success and failure in life. Below are some common self-sabotaging behaviours. How many do you relate to?

NOTE: Behaviours marked with an asterisk are the ones society regards as virtues! Be extra careful with these as they are still self-sabotaging techniques.

- *Procrastination* – leading to missed deadlines and opportunities

- *Inaction* – doing nothing achieves nothing

- *Laziness* – same as above and also makes a bad impression

- *Tardiness* – people will just get fed up of waiting for you and move on

- *Messiness* – leading to disorganisation, lost documents, bad image etc.

- *Chaos/chaotic lifestyle* – leads to a lack of stability from which to build future success and happiness

- *Drama* – unnecessary conflict, leading to loss of jobs, friends and partners

- **Perfectionism* – remember, done is better than perfect! Just let it go.

- *Negative self-talk* – you talk yourself down and belittle yourself

- *Envy* – you are too busy focusing on what others are doing to achieve anything yourself.

- *Narcissism* – thinking too well of yourself means that you wait for everything to be handed to you on a plate, because you're so special. You're not and it won't be! Life will just pass you by.

- *Substance abuse* – you cannot achieve anything if you are lost in a mental haze.

- *Drains* – gambling, shopping, pornography, internet scrolling - anything which misdirects your time, energy and money.

- **Selflessness/Martyrdom* – living life entirely for other people, with no life of your own

Learning to identify the moment you move into self-sabotaging behaviours is crucial, because then you can nip it in the bud before it derails your plans completely. While it isn't always easy to admit that you can be your own worst enemy, ignoring the fact only leads to the eventual collapse of your plans, so it is much better to be honest with yourself, keeping a check on self-sabotaging behaviours so that they don't get out of hand.

WHY DO WE SELF-SABOTAGE?

Everyone has some kind of self-sabotaging pattern. We all do it in one form or another. Whether you overeat, under achieve, over spend, procrastinate, pick fights or something else, we all have this tendency to derail our own progress. Why is this? Well, it is because self-sabotage of any kind is a skewed form of protection. You might want to make changes in your life, but the subliminal *fear of change*, triggers your pattern of negative habits, leading to self-sabotage. Most people have some degree of resistance to change, because it stems from the primal fear of the unknown, which is an innate part of our survival instincts.

Remember that your self-sabotaging habits have been a part of your life for a very long time, possibly even since childhood. This effectively means that they are so familiar to you, that breaking those patterns feels like an actual threat, so a degree of resistance is entirely natural. It's that uncomfortable comfort zone again. Furthermore, your brain works by calling on past experiences to address your current situation. In this way it can work on automatic pilot every time you drive a car, or make a cup of tea. You don't need to think about it, you just do it automatically. This is as true for your negative patterns as it is for more positive ones. You don't think about them, you just do them.

Some people feel a deep resistance to any kind of change at all, even if the changes they are being asked to make are beneficial ones. For instance, a smoker might say they want to quit, but often they have a deep resistance to giving up cigarettes. They might even go so far as to hide a secret stash, just in case! This is classic self-sabotaging behaviour, because as soon as they have a bad day, they are likely to retrieve the secret stash of cigarettes and start smoking again. Sabotage!

SIMPLE SELF-CARE: PATTERN INTERRUPT

Once you have identified your negative patterns and self-sabotaging behaviours, you need to interrupt them so that they don't derail your progress. When you notice that you are self-sabotaging, use a technique called the Pattern Interrupt, which is a way of over-riding your brain's habitual response by interrupting its normal route. So when you feel yourself reaching for another biscuit in the middle of your diet, interrupt that pattern by reaching for your pet instead, or a book to read, or tying your shoelaces. Keep your hands busy in a new way, and reprogram your mind to reach for something else, in order to break the habit. If you are in the habit of self-neglect, just go and turn the shower on. That's it, just turn it on and stand back, because as soon as you feel the steam on your face, you will want to get in! Another thing you might try is wearing an elastic band on your wrist and giving it a twang every time you notice yourself repeating a negative pattern of behaviour, or when you think you are about to self-sabotage. The momentary pain of the elastic twanging against your skin will help to interrupt the automatic negative pattern, giving you a chance to reprogram your mind with something more positive.

WITCHY WAYS: RELEASE YOUR RESISTANCE

This is a simple fire spell which will help you to shed any resistance you have towards positive change. All you need is a note pad and pen, a cauldron or heatproof dish and a lighter. Sit quietly and think about what needs to improve in your life and in your self-care. Can you feel any resistance to what needs to be done? If so, write it down on the note pad. You can write down the answers to the following questions if it helps, or write something else instead.

- *I am resistant because…*

- *I self-sabotage by…*

- *My fear is that…*

- *I worry that…*

- *My concern is…*

- *I would feel better if…*

Read through what you have written and see how it resonates with you. Reflect on those insights for a time, then when you feel ready, roll up the sheet of paper, set light to it and watch it burn in the cauldron as you say:

Resistance is natural, though it serves me not

Therefore, I release it, its power to rot

By ashes and dust, by fire and flame

I am free of resistance: I break from its chain.

GUARD YOUR SUBLIMINAL TONGUE!

Your internal voice is extremely powerful and it can have a profound impact on how you feel. The things you say to yourself each day, colour your outlook on life and your general wellbeing, so it is vital that your self-talk is positive because it is a key component in your mental and emotional wellbeing. Not only that, but you are a self-fulfilling prophecy, meaning that the things you focus on the most are what you attract into your life. For example, if you are looking for love, but you keep telling yourself that all prospective partners are bad eggs, then guess what kind of people you are attracting into your orbit? That's right - all the rotten ones! This reinforces your original belief that all people are bad eggs, and so the negative cycle continues.

The internal monologue you have with yourself is one of the most important aspects of self-care, because you simply won't feel happy and positive if you keep telling yourself how rubbish you are! Furthermore, it is perhaps the most accessible tool you have at your disposal, because no matter how unmotivated or drained you might be feeling, you always have the power to give yourself a little pep-talk. It takes very little energy, so you can do it even when you are at rock bottom, or sick or exhausted.

Positive self-talk is free, while negative self-talk will cost you dearly. It will rob you of your self-esteem, motivation, productivity, ambition, purpose and emotional stability. Even worse, it lowers your overall standards of what to expect from other people, meaning that someone might treat you badly and you believe that it's your fault, or that you deserve it. When you are in the habit of insulting and under-valuing yourself on a daily basis, it can be hard to accept that other people view you in quite a different way!

So what is self-talk and how does it support or hinder your self-care journey? Basically, self-talk is the inner voice of your mind. Have you ever been alone in the house and thought to yourself something along the lines of *"Let's have a cup of tea, I'll put the kettle on."* That is your inner voice speaking and it is speaking directly to you. It chatters away non-stop from the moment you wake up to the time you go to sleep, pondering questions, ruminating on past experiences, criticising or encouraging, planning or plotting, scheming and dreaming. It influences the things you dream about, the quality of your relationships, your sense of possibility or limitation and so much more. Your personal identity is created, to a large extent, by the things you believe and say to yourself, so having control of this inner voice is essential. Many people suffer in silence, being unaware of how they talk to themselves and the damage that voice might be doing. If your self-talk is negative, you might find yourself thinking things like:

- *I'm so stupid*

- *I can't do anything right*

- *Nothing good ever happens to me*

- *I'm so unlucky*

- *I'm cursed!*

- *I'm not good enough*

- *I don't deserve this*

- *I will never be happy*

- *I never get what I want*

- *Everyone else is better than me*

- *Life is so hard*

When you are saying such things to yourself day in day out, you are programming your mind to expect the worst of all worlds! Then, as a self-fulfilling prophecy, you will attract events, people and situations that reinforce and confirm all your negative beliefs. Consistent negative self-talk leads to low self-esteem and feelings of unworthiness, so it is vital that you get a grip on that inner voice, because it is a powerful tool that helps to create your reality. Be especially careful of how you speak about yourself to other people, even in jest, because saying negative things out loud makes them even more powerful. Self-deprecation is fine in very small doses, but don't let it become one of your self-sabotaging habits. The good news is that you can reprogram your mind with affirmations so that your self-talk becomes more positive.

AFFIRMATIONS

There are three different types of affirmation: spoken, written and action. Affirmations are positive statements or actions of intent and they are designed to over-ride negative though patterns and habits. When it comes to taking control of your self-talk, spoken affirmations are your new best friend! Using affirmations is like nurturing your self-worth so that in turn, you feel more positive and more capable. Even better, they are always available to you, no matter where you are or what you are doing. You can write your own affirmations or use the ones in this chapter. You can build several affirmations into larger statements of intent, or you can take a key word and repeat it like a mantra. It really is up to you. Say them in your head, or be bold and speak them out loud to your reflection in the mirror each morning. Try to memorise at least a few affirmations, the ones that resonate with you the most. That way you can use them anywhere.

SIMPLE SELF-CARE: USE AFFIRMATIONS
We have a lot of dead time in a day - waiting for a bus, commuting to work, showering, grocery shopping, soaking in the bath and so on. Use this dead time as a cue to start repeating your chosen affirmations. Say them out loud or in your head, but make sure you repeat them every day for the best results. Write them down each day if you want to create more of a ritual around your affirmations. Here are a few affirmations to get you started, but feel free to come up with your own.

- *I am enough*

- *I am worthy of love*

- *I love and respect myself*

- *I am worthy of the time it takes to look after myself*

- *I deserve to take care of myself and my home*

- *I always take care of my own needs*

- *I am strong and capable*

- *I deserve to be happy*

- *Good things come to me every day*

- *•I am very lucky and fortune smiles on me*

- *I am always in the right place at the right time*

- *I always have help when I need it*

- *I am entitled to happiness and joy*

- *•I deserve stability and wellbeing*

- *I believe in possibility*

- *I achieve all my goals and I can make my dreams come true*

- *Positive change is always an option*

- *I can change for the better*

THE TRICKERY OF TREATS

Self-sabotage can often masquerade as treats and sometimes our bad habits and negative patterns seem to come upon us out of the blue, though in reality that is rarely the case. The *awareness* comes out of the blue, but the habit was developed over time. You might go from having a glass of wine at the weekends, to suddenly realizing that you are drinking more alcohol throughout the week than your body can cope with, leaving you feeling lethargic and at risk of alcoholism. Beware of *treat* mentality because it can lead to bigger problems further down the line, such as over-spending, over-eating, addictions and so on. That is not to say that you should never treat yourself, but make sure the concept of a treat isn't masking a deep seated form of self-sabotage.

DEEPER HEALING: QUESTION YOURSELF

Questioning yourself about your bad habits is a good way to get to the bottom of the root cause of why they developed in the first place. Once you have identified the root cause, you can begin to deal with it, say in journalling, counselling or with other professional help. People who are dealing with addictions, for instance, can often trace the root cause back to a loss or trauma of some kind. Addressing this trauma removes the reason for their self-medicating, meaning that they can then, in turn, address the secondary issue of the addiction itself. You might already know the root cause of your negative habits if you did the mind mapping exercise from previously. However, questioning yourself can help you to dig deeper into your psyche and your core beliefs surrounding the issue. Answer the following questions in your journal to gain more insight into your situation.

- *How did I get here?*

- *What or who brought me to this place?*

- *Was it gradual or sudden?*

- *When did it truly begin?*

- *How long have I been thinking this way?*

- *What action did I take to begin this habit or lifestyle?*

- *Why am I behaving this way and where does that behaviour come from?*

- *Was there a catalyst for it, such as trauma or bereavement?*

- *Have I addressed that catalyst?*

- *If not, why not and what can I do to take steps to address it now?*

- *Is this habit filling some kind of void in my life?*

- *How can I better fill that void in a more positive way?*

- *Can I plant a new seed for a new, brighter future today?*

- *Can I change for the better and how? If not, why not, what stops me?*

This can be a difficult exercise to get through, but it is a very powerful tool of self-excavation. Try to make sure that there is someone within calling distance as you work through these questions and take it slow. You don't need to answer them all at once. Just take one or two questions at a time and work your way down the list, answering as fully and as honestly as you can, noting your responses in your journal, along with any physical sensations you experience during the exercise, i.e. flashbacks, emotional turmoil, anger, shivers, aches and pains. Note it all down. Afterwards do something enjoyable, such as the following exercise, to reset your mind to a happier place.

SIMPLE SELF-CARE: TASK BUILDING

When psychotherapists talk about task building, we are referring to stacking up positive habits in order to create a routine that is good for your wellbeing. Based on everything you have learnt so far in this book, start task building to create a positive daily routine. For instance, the tasks that form the survival level of self-care, when performed daily, will become your regular morning routine, so use this as a starting point. Now add in three more tasks from other sections of this book, or come up with your own, to incorporate throughout the rest of the day. You might include journalling, walking and affirmations to your routine, building those tasks into your daily life. You might want to focus more on the pampering aspects of self-care, adding in aromatherapy oils, a face mask and a soak in the bath. Perhaps you could create a calming night time routine, building in tasks such as meditation, art therapy, a long chat with a loved one or spending time with a pet. Think about when you will do the new tasks and how they will fit around your responsibilities and energy levels. Just pick three tasks to start with and build them into your daily routine.

SIMPLE SELF-CARE: BLOCK THE DRAINS

Now that you are more aware of your negative habits you will have a clear idea of where your personal drains are. Remember, a drain is anything that takes up your time and resources, without any real benefit, or to your detriment i.e. shopping, gambling, scrolling excessively and so on. Locate the source of your drains and take steps to block them. This could mean deleting your card details from online shopping sites and closing accounts. It could mean unsubscribing from content creators who trigger you or from sites that literally drain you, such as gambling sites. Or maybe you need to detach yourself from toxic groups of people. Whatever and wherever your personal drains are, take the necessary steps to block them today.

CHAPTER 5

WHAT'S YOUR STORY?

In the last chapter, we looked at how negative self-talk can lower your confidence and self-esteem. In this chapter we are going to dig a little deeper to discover your personal life story, which is known in psychotherapy as your *script*. The stories that you tell yourself have a significant impact on your mental health, emotional stability and the quality of life you lead. Just as belittling yourself keeps you small, a negative internal story-board can hold you back and stop you from achieving your dreams, prevent healing from trauma or overcoming loss. Your script is where you will find many of the root issues that present themselves in your day to day behaviour and mental health, such as depression, anxiety, fears, phobias and so on.

Learning more about your internal script can help you to overcome negative patterns of behaviour because you will have a better idea of their origins within your personal story. It can also highlight any blocks you may have developed in relation to self-care. Perhaps your script is telling you that pampering is an indulgence you cannot afford, for example, or that beauty will make you a target.

This type of self-excavation into your personal script can be a lot of fun, as you uncover the characters you relate to and how you might have assigned certain characters to those people who have played a significant role in your life. Are you forever falling in love with the big, bad wolf, for instance, or are you more of a sleeping beauty who is constantly self-sabotaging with inaction and procrastination? Maybe you're the ugly sister to your glamorous sibling? Whatever you script might be, it exists deep in your subconscious and although you might not be aware of it, it informs all your decisions. So what exactly is it and where did it come from?

EVERYONE HAS A STORY

Everyone has their own story. *Sonder* is a word that was coined by John Koenig for his online *Dictionary of Obscure Sorrows*, and is used to describe the acknowledgement that each individual is living out both the internal and external script of their life. Have you ever watched busy traffic during rush hour and wondered about the people in the various cars – where they are going, who might be waiting for them at home, what they are going to have for dinner that evening? This is *sonder* at work, as you silently acknowledge that the commuters are living busy lives that you will never know about and can only guess at, but you acknowledge it anyway. Over time, this acknowledgement leads to a deeper level of empathy with friends and strangers alike.

Your own story plays out in two ways, externally and internally. The external script involves getting up, getting dressed, going to work, paying bills, buying groceries, looking after the children and pets and so on. It is the things we all have to do every day, the mundane activities which make up the bulk of your life. The internal script plays out in your beliefs, patterns, self-talk, habits, routines, relationships and how well you care for yourself. It is perhaps the most powerful aspect of your story, because it determines how you view the world and move within it.

WHERE DOES YOUR SCRIPT COME FROM?

Your story, or script, is something that was formed in early childhood, when you learned what you had to do to survive. Children are extremely vulnerable, needing adults to protect, provide and care for them. However, a child's thinking process isn't rational. It makes a lot of generalisations and involves polarity thinking, where everything is black and white. This means that children as young as four or five years old, are constantly adapting their behaviour to ensure their own safety, so that their needs are being met, and this is how the script begins to take shape.

One example would be that of a little girl with a very flirtatious mother. The girl depends on her mother for everything. If the mother abandons the child, or neglects her, then the child believes she will starve and die. As the child grows up, in order to ensure her own survival, she becomes increasingly aware that she must never be viewed as a threat or rival to her mother. If she receives too much attention, the mother might abandon her, so the child remains small and quiet, trying not to draw attention to herself. She allows her mother to continue to shine, knowing that there isn't space for two flirtatious females in the same family - that role has already been taken by the mother. The pay-off for adopting this story is that is that the child maintains a harmonious relationship with her mum. Problems may arise as the child grows into adolescence and boys begin to take an interest in her. This could lead to a power struggle between mother and daughter, as one feels threatened and the other feels stifled.

This is a classic ugly duckling storyline, where the child has to suppress her own attractiveness so as not to pose a threat to her mother. This kind of script can play out in later life as feelings of not being good enough, preferring not to be the centre of attention, using self-neglect or even self-mutilation in an attempt to become less attractive, as the individual tries to remain in the shadows in order to keep her mother's love.

WHY YOUR SCRIPT IS IMPORTANT

Your script is a powerful component of your subconscious and it takes a lot of self-excavation work to uncover it and learn how your day to day life is impacted by it. From a very young age, you will have decided the life you were going to lead in adulthood, choosing poverty or prosperity, companionship or solitude, love or hate, peace or conflict, all in accordance with your surroundings at that time, and what the pay-off might have been. These decisions are carried through into adulthood, even though they no longer serve you in the same way and might even be holding you back. In general, your story will fall into one of three categories, as follows.

The Winning Script – People who develop a winning story tend to be high achievers who accomplish their goals. They choose happiness, gratitude and have an optimistic outlook on life. They tend to believe that things happen *for* them and that they are naturally lucky. Winning scripts include heroics, acts of service, courage, capability and openness. If as a child you always wanted to be Superman, Wonder Woman, a soldier or police officer, saving the world on a daily basis, this is a classic winning script.

The Losing Script – By contrast, someone with a losing script is likely to have a very negative outlook on life. They might complain at lot, lead a chaotic lifestyle or be a bit of a drama queen. They believe that life is out to get them and that they are a victim of bad luck. Losing scripts include risky behaviour, thrill seeking, chasing adrenalin highs, a lack of responsibility and personal accountability. This story tends to play out as a chaotic lifestyle, massive self-sabotage, living for the moment, unnecessary conflict, addictions, loss and under-achieving.

The Banal Script – A person with a banal script tends to live an unremarkable life, being neither a great success nor an under-achiever. This is the story of someone who plods through life, doing just enough to get by, but not enough to excel. They might get there eventually, but the accolades are few and far between. They are the tortoise in the fable of *The Tortoise and the Hare*. Banal scripts include a lack of self-motivation and a moderate amount of self-sabotage, but not usually enough to derail them completely. People with this kind of script tend to experience very safe, small lives, with little to no excitement, which can often feel claustrophobic and stifling.

SIMPLE SELF-CARE: ARE YOU WINNING, LOSING OR BANAL?

Think back over your life and try to identify the patterns and how they might come from your subconscious script. What story have you been telling yourself since childhood? Are you afraid to succeed because your father was an under-achiever, or do you feel the need to excel in all things in order to keep parental approval? Bear in mind that this isn't about blaming your parents for how your life has turned out. It is simply about digging deep into your own psyche so that you can begin to pinpoint the story you needed to tell yourself in childhood, in order to get your needs met. Is your personal story one of winning, losing or somewhere in between? Note down any insights you might have had with regard to your script. Does it drive you forward, hold you back or keep your life small and safe? How might you change or improve this script to a more winning one?

STORYTIME

There are more obvious places to look for clues as to what your personal script might be and that is in books and movies. Sometimes you might identify so strongly with a particular character, that it can feel as if you are witnessing an alternate version of your own life story. In a way that is exactly what is happening, for we each have our own personal myth which gradually unfolds as we make our way through life. If you pick up a book or watch a movie that resonates with your inner mythology and life script, it can have a profound effect and leave a lasting impression. Excavating this story from your subconscious and bringing it to the surface of

your mind can help you to rise to life's challenges and develop a
more positive outlook.

DEEPER HEALING: TEACHING TALES

The idea of using stories as teaching tools is far from new. Moral
tales and parables can be found in all cultures and religions, in all
parts of the world. The psychologist C G Jung used fairy tales
and mythology to understand the complex workings of the mind
and how we relate to specific archetypes. His concepts are still
used in modern therapy. Today's social workers will often use dolls
to gain the trust of a child who has been traumatized in some way,
encouraging the child to play out the trauma using the dolls as a
story telling device. This is far more than child's play, for as Clarissa
Pinkola Estes states in her book *Women Who Run with the Wolves*
'Stories are medicine' and they can have a healing effect upon a
troubled mind.

Stories can lift the spirits: inspire courage and valour: sooth the
soul: open the heart to romance and love: offer warnings and alert
you to possible danger: raise aspirations and put you in the mood
for an adventure. When you surrender to the escape of a good
book and lose yourself in the story, you are also tapping into your
own personal myth and an aspect of your life script.

Sometimes this deeply hidden myth will link back to a particular
fairy tale, as these are the very first stories we are told and the
first characters we relate to. Reading fairytales as an adult is a
completely different experience to the bedtime stories you enjoyed
as a child, especially if you pay close attention to the magical
symbolism within the tales. Clues to your personal gifts, strengths
and challenges can be found in your favourite fairy tale, thus
encouraging you to play to your strengths and overcome the
challenge, as depicted in the table below. This effectively means
that your favourite fairytale is linked to your internal script. What
does it tell you about your story?

FAIRYTALE	THE GIFT	THE CHALLENGE
Sleeping Beauty	an initiation/rebirth	tendency to dream
Cinderella	transcendence	poverty/struggle
Beauty & the Beast	to see beneath appearances	can be judgemental
The Frog Prince	to see the best in people	easily mislead
Rapunzel	autonomous strength	unsociable/isolated
Red Riding Hood	independent spirit	trusts wrong people
Snow Queen	adventurous spirit	can be cold/aloof
Swan Maiden	gentleness/purity	fears lost innocence
Ugly Duckling	self-acceptance	doesn't fit in

BARDS, TROUBADOURS AND MINSTRELS

In the past, story telling was an art form that was highly regarded. This was especially so in Celtic and Druidic traditions. At the end of each day, families and clan would gather together around a huge fire, and troubadour tales of heroes and adventure would be told. This was an oral tradition - tales had to be carefully memorized, for few people could read or write, so stories were verbally passed down through the generations. Out of this oral tradition came much of what we now know as the Norse Sagas, Arthurian Legend, Celtic, Greek and Roman mythology, and of course the popular fairy tales we are all familiar with.

But what is it about stories that so intrigues us? And why were the old story tellers, such as bards and troubadours, held in such high esteem? Perhaps it is because stories enable us to take a mental journey to far off places and other worlds, to see our own world in a new and different way: in short, to escape for a while. It could also be that stories have the power to inspire us, while myths and legends introduce us to the world of magic. In this sense the story tellers themselves become the magicians.

Even today best-selling authors can achieve a high celebrity status and become house hold names. Think of writers such as Philippa Gregory, Terry Pratchett, Dan Brown and Barbara Erskine. Such authors are our modern day tribal story tellers and society still places them in a position of honour. Perhaps the most well-known poets and story tellers of history were the great bards of the Druid tradition. Today's Druids still follow an oral tradition, learning and memorizing their poems, sagas and rituals, largely without committing anything to paper.

In Wiccan tradition also, stories and poems are used in ritual and sabbat celebrations. Thus modern witches still make use of the tales of John Barleycorn and the Oak and Holly Kings, in order to better understand the laws of nature and the passing of the seasons. Such stories have become part of the foundation of modern witchcraft. Poems and popular fairy tales can also be used in this way, helping us to better understand ourselves and the world around us through symbolism, imagery and stereotype.

Such writings can also teach us more about the elementals and faeries, magic in general and the pagan goddess. To witches and magical practitioners' fairy tales are a valuable source of reference. Hidden within each popular fairy tale is a core of magic and pagan symbolism. This shouldn't be too surprising as most popular fairy tales have been in circulation, in one form or another, for hundreds of years.

SIMPLE SELF-CARE: FINDING YOUR PERSONAL MYTH
World mythology is full of powerful gods and goddesses. From Apollo, Cernunnos, Arawn and Herne to Persephone, Demeter, Venus, Aphrodite, Ceres and the Cailleach: all cultures present divine archetypes within their mythology. Such legendary icons are a great place to begin uncovering your own personal mythology. Is there a particular deity who resonates with you and whom you regard as your patron: does their story hold a special significance for you? Does this myth tie in with your favourite fairytale or your life script? Let's say for example, that your chosen fairytale is Red Riding Hood and your patron goddess is Persephone: both these stories refer to abduction, betrayal and trickery, so your personal myth would be one of learning to trust your instincts, rather than accepting the friendly prattle of a stranger.

Finding your personal myth is an excavation of your deep subconscious: it is a process of continually asking yourself *'Why did I enjoy that film so much? Why do I keep coming back to this book, this goddess, this protagonist?'* Look for the parallels which link together the books, films, art and music that you most enjoy. Look also, for the parallels which link these stories to events in your own life. Try to find the storylines which tie them all together and you will discover that your own myth and life script is also woven within the fabric of the tales. In this way you can learn from the protagonist's mistakes, avoid the pitfall of your mythology and become a stronger version of yourself.

WHO IS YOUR HEROINE?

Another tip for discovering your myth is to look to your heroes and heroines. Whether these are fictional characters or people from history, the person you hold as your hero or heroine tells a lot about you. Do you admire a sporting legend who won against all odds: or a great orator and thinker who changed the world for the better? Perhaps you gain strength from the victory of an ancient warrior such as William Wallace or the feisty Boudicca? Once again, look for the parallels which link your hero or heroine to your own life story and see what you can learn from her. What are they telling you about your personal myth: where are you most likely to meet with the challenge your myth presents, and how would your hero deal with such a situation? In this way you can tap into the strength of say, Boudicca, in order to overcome difficult situations in your own life. Once you come to understand your personal mythology and how your script informs your current life, you will come to understand yourself on a much deeper level. In this way you can begin to ensure that you face life from a position of greater strength. *You* are the troubadour, your life is your story and *happy ever after* is yours for the taking!

DEEPER HEALING: CHANGE YOUR STORY, CHANGE YOUR LIFE

One of the first steps to improving your life is to become more aware of when you are acting from your personal script. You might go through life distrustful, pushing people away because your script equates safety with solitude, or you may become a spendthrift because you believe that people will only be interested in you for your wealth. Having this awareness of how your script influences your habits and behaviours on a daily basis is crucial, because you must learn to over-ride this conditioning from early childhood.

Whatever your script has been up to now, know that you can change your life by starting to tell yourself a different story. Remember that the ugly duckling was destined to grow into a swan, not remain a duckling who didn't quite fit in! Your script is an illusion and it is in your power to change it for something more positive, so pick a story that serves you better.

CHAPTER 6
WHAT DRIVES YOU?

Your script is only one form of conditioning that takes place in early childhood that can have a strong impact on how you feel in your adult life. Another is your psychological drivers. These are the subliminal messages you received as a youngster from your parents and care-givers. Again, this happens at a deeply subconscious level and neither you nor your parents will be aware of developing, or passing on, these subliminal messages. Once again, your parents and care-givers are not at fault here. Drivers are just information which the child-mind absorbs, distorts and holds onto, meaning that these messages tend to play out throughout the course of your life, without you even being aware of it. They can have quite a negative impact though, so the sooner you can identify what your personal drivers are, the sooner you can begin to over-ride them.

WHAT ARE PSYCHOLOGICAL DRIVERS?

As the name suggests, psychological drivers are the subconscious urges that drive your current behaviour and they have been instilled into your mind since childhood. They are a natural extension of your personal script and they influence how you move through the world and interact with others.

You are likely to have more than one driver, as different care-givers influenced you in different ways from a very young age. This means that you will revert to different driver behaviours depending on who you are with and what the circumstances are. You might act from one driver when in the company of your father (or someone who reminds you of him), but from another driver when spending time with your mother or siblings and so on.

Psychological drivers can have a very negative impact on your health and mental wellbeing. They are essentially the triggers we don't usually know we have, but they constantly trigger our behaviour every single day. Discovering your drivers therefore, is crucial to getting out of the *scripted* kind of behaviour you adopted as a child and which we looked at in the previous chapter.

Some of these drivers will be very familiar and you might already know that they are not good. Perfectionism, for instance, is a psychological driver. So is people pleasing. On the surface these look like virtues and society conditions you to believe that they are, but over time, both these psychological drivers can leave you feeling exhausted, not good enough and guilty for no reason. Hint: if you struggle to say no to people, then you probably have at least one of these drivers. Let's take a closer look at the five main psychological drivers and how they can influence your behaviour and affect your wellbeing.

BE PERFECT

Perfectionism is a very common driver. It is the bane of many people's lives, yet it is often held aloft as something to strive for. This is especially the case if you work in the military or emergency services, where mistakes can cost lives. As perfectionists often like to remind us, *there's always room for improvement!* Is there really though? Not always. For example, no matter how many eggs you crack, not one of them is going to break in a perfectly straight line, is it?

Perfectionism isn't a virtue! It is a psychological driver that can leave you feeling as if nothing you do is ever good enough. It can make someone very difficult to live with and prone to expecting unachievably high standards from their loved ones and the people around them.

SIMPLE SELF-CARE: OVERRIDE THE 'BE PERFECT' DRIVER
If you are a perfectionist, stop claiming it as one of your virtues, as this only adds to the psychological damage. Instead, challenge yourself to do something imperfectly, to leave a task half done, or to allow some untidiness into your life. It's impossible to be perfect all the time, so why keep setting yourself up to fail? Learn to get comfortable with your own short-comings and try not to expect perfection from others. Just learn to let things go a little bit.

BE STRONG

Like perfectionism, a be-strong driver can often be mistaken for a virtue, and it can certainly help you to get through difficult times. Someone with a be-strong driver is the kind of person who keeps their head in a crisis. They are calm, capable, reliable, helpful and can always be called upon for assistance. They may pride themselves on being able to cope with anything life hurls their way, taking set-backs in their stride and somehow, always managing to get back on their feet quite quickly. Nothing keeps someone with a be-strong driver down for long! Their bounce-back ability is second to none.

Of course, there are downsides to this. It can be difficult for someone with this driver to ask for help when they need it, or to accept help when it is offered. It can mean that they are viewed as the *rock* of the family, with everyone else leaning on them for support. They tend to take on all the hard jobs in the family too, such as visiting sick relatives, caring for elderly parents and arranging funerals etc. They are the mainstay of their family, friends and colleagues. Until they break.

When a be-strong personality eventually breaks, it is usually fairly catastrophic, leading to mental breakdowns, suicidal thoughts, conditions such as PTSD and panic attacks, self-medicating and possibly addiction. Often, the breakdown will happen sometime after the event that triggered it, meaning that it comes out of the blue for all involved. You might not even link the two events in your mind. This is as true for an episode of tears and tantrums, as it is for more significant breakdowns. It generally happens long after the dust has settled, taking everyone by surprise, not least the person who is used to being strong, capable and able to cope with anything! But even the strongest bridge will collapse under too much pressure.

SIMPLE SELF-CARE: OVERRIDE THE 'BE STRONG' DRIVER

If you are driven by your own inner strength, bear in mind that you cannot and should not, take the weight of the world on your shoulders. Also, try not to expect other people to cope as well as you do. They are not weak: they just have a different psychological driver from you.

Be careful how much assistance you give to others and protect your energy as much as possible. Identify the drains, making sure that you are helping people who are prepared to help themselves, rather than sending all your energy to draining people who can't be bothered with their own life.

As tempting as it might be, you can't go through life all alone, without ever needing the support of other people around you. You deserve support too. Learn to ask for help when you need it, even if it's just asking someone else to wash the car for you. Let people help you. You don't have to carry all the burdens, all the time, all by yourself. Delegate!

TRY HARD

There is no doubt that people who never try, never get anywhere, but trying too hard can be bad for your mental health. People with a try-hard driver like to pride themselves on the fact that they never give up, that they get there in the end, or that they gave it their very best shot. All of this sounds very virtuous, but there *is* such a thing as trying *too* hard, and that is exactly what this driver can lead you to do. Try-hard types can come across as being quite desperate. Trying too hard in your romantic relationships means that you may be accused of being clingy. Trying too hard in your friendships can also seem quite needy. In general, desperation pushes people away, because it's just too intense.

The other danger for people with a try hard driver is that they frequently fail to adapt. They are so single minded and focused on their goal, that they will try and try and try again, but never think to take a step back and find a fresh approach. They just keep chipping away at the same rock face, wondering why they haven't discovered any diamonds yet! Albert Einstein famously said that the definition of insanity is doing the same thing over and over, and expecting a different result. He could have been talking about someone with a try-hard psychological driver!

There is nothing wrong with trying to get ahead, trying to achieve something, or making an effort, but the downside to this driver is that it can lead you to wasting significant amounts of time, *trying* for things that are clearly not working. A good example is that of someone in a relationship that has deteriorated beyond repair. Both partners might be very unhappy, but only one of them wants to break free and start fresh, while the other wants to keep trying and trying and trying, regardless of the fact that this will only prolong the misery on both sides.

A try-hard driver can lead to someone wasting years of their life in negative situations, as they *try desperately* to turn it into a positive. This is classic try-hard behaviour, toxic positivity and a form of self-sabotage. You have to know when to give up and move on. Or at least, find another way.

SIMPLE SELF-CARE: OVERRIDE THE 'TRY HARD' DRIVER
If you have a try-hard driver, it will be very difficult for you to let things go. You will never accept defeat and will keep going until you drop! This is only a virtue if you are getting the results you want, otherwise, as Einstein said, it's a form of madness. Learn to take a step back from the situation. Do something else for a while, go away and distract yourself. With the benefit of distance, you might realize that you don't actually *want* whatever it is you were trying for after all. Or you might come up with a more inspired action and another approach to achieve your goal. Giving yourself space to think is the first step to achieving clarity, so stop wasting time in trying, step back and look for an alternative route. Substitute *trying* for doing something else instead.

PLEASE OTHERS

Another very common driver is that of the people pleaser. People with a please-others driver will often put their own needs last, as they cater to everyone else around them first. People-pleasers are the sacrificial lambs to the slaughter of life. This is the classic martyr mindset at work. It looks amazing on the surface, as people might tell you how wonderful you are at spinning plates and juggling so many responsibilities, but in reality, it is a slow road to burn out. Signs of a please-others driver include taking on too much at once, feeling pressured into doing things you'd rather not do, being taken advantage of, carrying the responsibilities of other people and volunteering for extra jobs when you already have enough on your plate. People with a please-others driver find it very difficult to say no, to anyone, in any situation. This means that they can find themselves out of their depth - sexually, professionally and morally. They always want to make others happy, to make their lives easier, to be liked and this leads to people-pleasers being taken for granted, used and abused. In extreme cases, it can lead to dangerous situations or being caught up in criminal activity, because they find it impossible to say no to things that make them uncomfortable. A please-others driver can lead someone to act against their own conscience, losing their moral centre, resulting in self-hatred and loathing.

SIMPLE SELF-CARE: OVERRIDE THE 'PLEASE OTHERS' DRIVER

If you have a please others driver you tend to sacrifice aspects of yourself in order to do what other people want. This could mean that you sacrifice your integrity to tell lies for a friend, or you might sacrifice your sexual comfort to experiment with a partner in ways that you later regret. The main issue with this driver is that you cannot say no and so your boundaries (if you have any!) are constantly being tested, eroded and breached. You tend to follow the crowd, going along with whatever everyone else wants to do, for the sake of a quiet life. The please others driver also indicates that you fear conflict, have difficulty in standing up for yourself and can be a bit of a doormat.

You don't have to try and please everyone. Make the decision to start pleasing yourself for a change. Stand up for yourself more. Learn to say no. Define your own boundaries and decide what is acceptable to you and what isn't, then stick to your guns. It can take a while to get out of the habit of being everyone's doormat, but a good first step is to start biting them on the ankles whenever they try to walk all over you!

HURRY UP!

The hurry-up driver masquerades as busyness and we live in a world where being extremely busy is considered a wonderful achievement in its own right! Someone with a hurry-up driver is never still. They cannot remain in one place for more than five minutes and they often feel very guilty for doing anything relaxing, such as reading a book or watching a film, as they believe that they should be busy doing something more productive instead.

Toxic productivity is a key component of this psychological driver and hurry-up types like to have long to-do lists, multiple jobs and hobbies, lots of places to go and people to see. Their life is one constant round of activity and things to do, though they are not necessarily high achievers. They often lack the stillness, focus and commitment to see a goal through to manifestation. They move swiftly from one task to another, to the next and so on. They might even find it difficult to relax while on holiday, creating a list of things to see and do while abroad, when their body is crying out for poolside rest and rejuvenation.

Often highly stressed, fast-talking fidgets, people with a hurry-up driver are easily distracted from the task at hand. Ironically, they also tend to be very bad at time management, frequently arriving late and keeping people waiting, or showing up very early and taking everyone by surprise. This is because they are trying to do a million things at once, or they don't have the patience to wait until the appointed time slot, or they get distracted by something just as they are about to leave the house, which makes them late for appointments and meetings etc. They also mistake busyness for being high achievers, but these are two very different things and they don't always go hand in hand!

SIMPLE SELF-CARE: OVERRIDE THE 'HURRY UP' DRIVER
If you have a hurry-up driver you will expect the rest of the world to move at *your* pace – if you are late for a meeting you expect

everyone to wait for you, if you are early, you expect people to still be ready for you. Basically, you expect the world to drop everything for you at a moment's notice! Of course, when this doesn't happen, you can feel quite frustrated and may blame others for your bad time keeping!

It can be very hard to around someone who is motivated by a hurry up driver, because everything they do is so fast! It's exhausting. Understand that everyone has their own pace, their own way of doing things. In the meantime, if this is your driver, you need to make a concerted effort to just slow down. Allow yourself time to relax and rest. Rest is important. It lowers stress levels, blood pressure and decreases the heart rate. Going through life at a mile a minute is bad for your health, so take your time. Enjoy your surroundings. Look at the view. Stop and smell the roses! Monitor your time management and see what improvements can be made. Are you under-estimating how long it takes you to get ready, for instance, or how long the journey into work is? See where you can adjust your routine, so that you are not rushing to do things, but so that tasks are still accomplished in a timely manner, at a steady pace. Don't forget to breathe. Just breathe. It's good for you.

RESPECT YOUR DRIVERS (BUT DON'T LET THEM RULE YOU!)

As you can see, your psychological drivers play a key role in your day to day life. They are a part of your personality. In small doses they can be beneficial, helping you to achieve goals, endure tough times and make new friends. If you allow yourself to be ruled by your drivers, however, they can become quite toxic. Every driver has the potential to lead to self-sabotaging behaviours, so it is important that you keep them in check.

While you will never eliminate them from your personality, becoming more aware of them means that you can use these triggers to your advantage, rather than have them work against you. Bear in mind that we all have a least some of these drivers. Often we move through the drivers at random, depending on the circumstance in which we find ourselves, but one or two drivers will be far more dominant in your personality, with the remaining three only coming into play when the situation calls for them. You might have dominant be-strong and try-hard drivers all the time, but then tip into please-others when you are at a social event, for instance.

DEEPER HEALING: BECOME AWARE OF YOUR DRIVERS
Recognizing and identifying your personal drivers is crucial in living a contented life, because if you don't recognize them, they have the power to sabotage and derail you completely. Self-awareness is the key, so to become more aware of your psychological drivers, try to find clues from your habits and self-talk. Are you always in a rush, or telling the kids they need to be quicker? This is a clue that you have a hurry-up driver. Do friends and family always turn to you for help and support? You probably have a be-strong driver. Are you constantly run off your feet because you have agreed to do several favours for friends, or overtime at work? That's a please-others driver at work.

Take a little time right now and think back over the past few days. What did you do, who did you talk to, did you make any agreements? What driver were you acting from in these situations? Your most dominant drivers are likely to be the easiest to identify because you use them every day and they are your MO. What other drivers can you find in your day to day life? Find them, recognize them and take steps to over-ride them when they begin to get out of hand.

CHAPTER 7
DRAMA KARMA

S elf-care begins with a deep self-awareness. If you don't monitor your own body, moods, habits and interactions, then you have no control over your life. A natural consequence of the deeper level of self-awareness you are learning from this book, is that you will also become more observant of just how rare self-awareness actually is.

Throughout the course of your daily life, you will have many interactions with people who have no self-awareness at all! Not everyone has the motivation or willingness to work on themselves, to confront their issues and put their best face forwards. Not everyone is ready for such a journey, and that's okay. You can't force people to evolve psychologically. It has to come from them.

Inevitably then, you will meet with people who have done no internal work at all, who carry their wounds and issues with them everywhere they go and who therefore interact from a very wounded place. This typically comes across as angry, aggressive behaviour, but not always. Sometimes it can present itself as general chaos, histrionic outbursts or very low self-esteem. Often though, it comes with a certain amount of drama attached, so how do you prevent this drama from seeping into your own life and psyche? In the midst of drama, how do you maintain the calmness of your self-care bubble? The answer is, you rise above it, but with compassion.

NOBLESSE OBLIGE

Noblesse oblige is a French expression which basically means that with privilege comes obligation. At the time, it referred to the privilege of wealth and the responsibility of the noble class to care for the lower class, by ensuring that they had work, homes, food etc. In modern vernacular, however, the term has been expanded to mean that anyone with any kind of privilege should extend kindness, compassion and consideration to those who are less privileged.

What does this mean in terms of self-care? In a nutshell, it means that you are in a privileged position to be able to care for yourself and work on your inner strength, overcoming issues and challenges along the way. Not everyone has this privilege, while some individuals are simply not ready for it.

Noblesse oblige means that when someone without self-awareness is acting out their pain in a dramatic manner, we make certain allowances and show them compassion. This is not about being condescending, or accepting aggressive or threatening behaviour. It is about being kind to people who, for whatever reason, do not have the same mental resilience and forbearance that you have. It is about demonstrating honourable conduct, even in challenging situations. Noblesse oblige means that you navigate areas of potential conflict with compassion, keeping yourself out of the drama as much as possible and above the fray.

WITCHY WAYS: NOBLESSE OBLIGE RITUAL
One the night of the full moon, take a pale blue candle and anoint it with lavender essential oil. As you do so, consider all the aspects of your life where there might be some drama. This could be at work, in your relationship or with family members. Consider the situation from their point of view. Could there be some underlying issue that you are not aware of, which is contributing to the drama? Place the anointed candle in a holder, take three deep breaths and

centre yourself. Remember the concept of noblesse oblige. Understand that you are in a privileged position to have witchcraft at your fingertips, to have a certain level of self-awareness and the motivation to work on your issues. Know that this privilege comes with a responsibility to forgive those who may not have such tools at their disposal. When you feel ready, light the candle and say:

In the spirit of noblesse oblige

I move through the world with grace

Situations may be oblique

Others move at their own pace

In loving light this candles shines

Its warmth will pave the way

Compassion is a gift divine

I share it every day.

CHAOTIC LIFESTYLES

Chaos is one of the most obvious indicators that someone is living in a very dramatic and histrionic way. We have all met people who seem to attract chaos. It follows them wherever they go. They always have a story to tell and this is usually a list of woes and complaints against the world. A chaotic lifestyle may mean that someone keeps losing jobs, homes, relationships and so on. While anyone can lose any one of these things through no fault of their own, if someone is losing them several times, over and over again, it is an indication that their life is ruled by drama. Often, they will try to draw other people into that drama, either by looking for a sounding board to complain to, a shoulder to cry on without end, or by blaming others for their situation.

Drama is largely self-generated. It can escalate quite quickly and it tends to attract more of the same. This is why people with dramatic personalities frequently end up in toxic relationships together! Like attracts like and drama can be very magnetic. When someone chooses drama as a lifestyle though, often that choice is made outside of their own awareness, which basically means that they cannot and will not accept that *they* are the problem! It can be very difficult to help someone with this type of mindset, because they will always blame other people for their problems, or complain that you do not understand the complexity of their situation and how powerless they are to improve it. So what are the signs that someone is acting from a place of drama and chaos? Below are some of the most common indicators.

- Constant complaining

- Unsettled lifestyle

- Erratic behaviour

- Can't hold down a job

- Histrionic outbursts

- Emotional incontinence

- Tantrums and other childish behaviour

- Blaming everyone else for their problems

- Refusing to address their problems or get help or counselling

- Picking fights and being argumentative

- Bad attitude

- Polarity thinking – everything is black or white, good or evil etc.

- Carrying historic drama – they hold onto every hurt and insult as if it just happened, frequently regurgitating the pain

- Bad time keeping (*especially* if they have a Hurry-Up driver!)

SIMPLE SELF-CARE: SEPARATE ISSUES FROM DRAMA
What do you do if you know someone who is living from a very chaotic and dramatic or histrionic mindset? Or if you recognize these tendencies in yourself? The most important thing you can do to address this kind of behaviour, in yourself or in others, is to learn how to separate the issue from the drama. The *issue* might be that someone has had a traumatic experience in the past, or they might be struggling with addiction, low self-esteem and so on. The *drama* that surrounds this issue is likely to present itself as a bad attitude, argumentative and aggressive behaviour, endless complaints and so on. Issues can be addressed in professional counselling, through journalling, or by reading books such as this one and taking its lessons on board. Getting straight to the heart of the problem and addressing the internal issue, means that given time, all the external drama will begin to fall away, because it was really just a red flag, meant to alert the individual that something wasn't right. Life will often give you hints when you're getting it wrong, but it's up to you to recognize those hints and act upon them in a positive, pro-active manner.

CATASTROPHIZING

Catastrophizing is when someone makes mountains out of molehills, turning small problems into big ones and generally making things out to be much worse than they actually are. This kind of behaviour goes hand in hand with a dramatic and chaotic lifestyle, so it likely that you will have witnessed it, or may even have been guilty of it yourself.

Assuming that the worst will always happen is extremely damaging to your mental health. Catastrophizing causes negative thought spirals, leading to anxiety, overwhelm, panic attacks and depression. That said, these very same conditions can also cause people to catastrophize, so it can be a bit of a conundrum!

It can be difficult to assume the best will happen if you have experienced some kind of trauma, because your mind draws on its past experiences to deal with current situations. Viewed in this light, it makes perfect sense that some traumatized people will catastrophize every situation in which they find themselves. But it is not a healthy way to live and it certainly won't enhance your self-care.

While catastrophizing isn't a mental health issue in and of itself, it is often a symptom of other issues such as PTSD, OCD, ADHD, addiction, extreme fatigue, chronic pain, illness and so on. Furthermore, it can make these conditions worsen and cause a serious flare up. Catastrophizing is just another reason why it pays to monitor your internal thoughts and self-talk, so that you can nip it in the bud before it takes hold.

SIMPLE SELF-CARE: STOP CATASTROPHIZING
Interrupting the pattern of catastrophic thoughts can take a while. If you have developed a habit of imagining the worst case scenario, then it will take some time to break that habit. Nevertheless, the sooner you begin to recalibrate your thoughts, the sooner you will no longer be held hostage by your catastrophic imaginings. Try to turn it into a game. As soon as you notice that you are thinking

of how bad things could be, ask yourself these questions:

- *What is the BEST that could possibly happen?*

- *What is the BENEFIT of this situation and how is it serving me?*

- *What is the SILVER LINING?*

- *Is there a LESSON here and what can I LEARN from this?*

- *Have I SURVIVED this kind of situation before? (You probably have!)*

- *Will I feel BETTER if I take a nap or a walk?*

- *Am I in immediate danger right now? (You're probably not!)*

- *What is the silliest, funniest outcome I can imagine with regard to this situation? Is that likely to happen?*

In working your way through these questions you are actually talking your mind down from the ledge. Imagining the funniest outcome will show you that, as unlikely as it is to happen, it is just as unlikely as the worst case scenario you've been torturing yourself with. Yes, the mind can play tricks, but you are in control of it, so make sure that your thought patterns are serving you well.

WITCHY WAYS: DARK CRYSTAL SPELL TO ABSORB CATASTROPHIZING THOUGHTS
First of all, remove yourself from the current situation and find a quiet space. Keep a black crystal, such as black obsidian or smoky quartz, with you if you know that you are prone to negative thought spirals. Once in your quiet place, take the crystal and hold it close

to your lips. Breathe out all the negative emotions, and visualize the dark crystal absorbing those energies. These darker crystals are very good for absorbing negativity and neutralizing it, so keep breathing your panic into the crystal until a state of calmness is restored. Immediately afterwards, rinse the crystal in cold running water to cleanse away all the negativity and make the crystal ready for next time you need it. As an alternative, if you don't have a black crystal handy, you can breathe the negative panic into a tissue and then flush it away.

THE DRAMA TRIANGLE

The Drama Triangle was the concept of psychoanalyst, Stephen Karpman and it is frequently used in all kinds of therapy, counselling and social work. The idea behind it is that every altercation revolves around the three positions of the triangle and they are: Victim, Persecutor and Rescuer. In a nutshell, this means that whenever you find yourself embroiled in some kind of drama or conflict, you will assume one of these positions and so will the person, or people, you are in conflict with. Here's how it works:

- *Persecutor – this is the person who is on the attack*

- *Victim – this is the person who feels they must defend themselves*

- *Rescuer – this person is springing to the defence of either the Victim OR the Persecutor (sometimes switching back and forth, as they try to see both sides of the argument) or acting as a kind of mediator, in which case, they are Rescuing the situation or the family dynamics.*

Karpman claimed that in every argument, the combatants would initially take up one position, but often they would switch to a different position on the Drama Triangle halfway through the argument, meaning that in any altercation, the participants are dancing round and round the triangle and nothing is ever resolved. Not only is this exhausting and repetitive, it is also damaging to relationships and to family and group dynamics. Signs that you are on the Drama Triangle include saying things like:

- *We're arguing round in circles and getting nowhere*

- *I'm sick of having this same discussion over and over*

- *Nothing ever changes, we just keep going over old ground*

You can see the Drama Triangle play out in any city centre on a Saturday night. Two lads might start to argue (Victim and Persecutor), then the friend of one lad butts in (trying to Rescue his mate), followed by two friends of the other lad (also trying to Rescue *their* mate), and before long there is a full scale brawl going on! This is usually when the police (Rescuer/Mediator), step in and break it up.

The Drama Triangle plays out in families, friend groups, workplaces and social situations all over the world. No-one is immune to it. It is universal. It's how wars break out between two countries (Persecutor and Victim, Invader and Occupied), with allied forces sent in to Rescue and Mediate, in order to bring about peace. Chances are that you will have some personal experience of being on this Triangle, though you might not have been aware of the dynamics in play at the time. Some people pick an aspect of the Triangle and become so comfortable there, that it becomes their MO. We see this in people who have a victim mentality, in bullies who love to persecute others and in those who are forever trying to rescue and save people from themselves. Obviously, it isn't a healthy way to interact. Fortunately, understanding how the Drama Triangle works means that you will be able to recognise when you have inadvertently stumbled into it and take steps to remedy the situation.

DEEPER HEALING: GETTING OFF THE DRAMA TRIANGLE

The Drama Triangle is by its very nature, dysfunctional and destructive. However, conflict is an aspect of life, so there is a strong chance that you will find yourself in the midst of a dramatic altercation at some point in time. When this happens, pause for a moment and try to identify the position you are being expected to take upon the Drama Triangle. Are you playing the Victim, Persecutor or Rescuer? None of these is a positive position, though Rescuer is possibly the most benign.

Opting out is the best course of action for you to take, so instead of playing the game someone else has set before you, simply make a conscious decision to withdraw from the Triangle altogether, and refuse to take on any of the roles it requires. Remember that just because someone invites you to an argument, that doesn't mean you have to accept the invitation! Rise above it, put your own mental health first, and walk away.

CHAPTER 8
THE ART OF SELF-SOOTHING

At its heart, self-care is about learning how to sooth yourself after a hard day, or when you feel the need for some extra TLC. As you have seen from previous chapters, you can often hold on to a lot of stress from your past and from unsavoury interactions with other people. That's just life. The problems begin to stack up when people don't know how to sooth themselves after a negative event, or when they feel guilty for wanting to pamper themselves and so they just don't bother.

I would argue that life is tough enough, without being hard on yourself! You need to become your own confidant, cheerleader, bodyguard and beauty therapist. You need to get comfortable wearing lots of different hats, because different situations call for a different response. Discovering that you can be your own first port of call can be quite eye-opening for some people, while others might need to learn how to ask for help more frequently.

Self-soothing is a term psychotherapists use with clients and it refers to the practice of offering yourself soft acts of kindness, especially when you are going through a tough time. It is about honouring your feelings, validating them and soothing the psychological wound, with acts of self-care. For instance, imagine that you had just fallen off a horse during a riding lesson. You're not injured and so you know the drill – you need to get back on the horse. This isn't your first rodeo! You finish your ride and go home, but for the remainder of the day, you feel a bit off kilter, a little down in the dumps, possibly even tearful. Why is this? Well, it is because you haven't really acknowledged the fall. You might take pride in the fact that you got back in the saddle, you might be grateful for the fact that were not injured during the fall, but none of that is particularly *soothing* to your soul or to your psychological self.

In such a situation then, how would you go about self-soothing? First of all, you need to acknowledge what just happened, then honour the emotions the event brought up, before offering yourself some soft acts of kindness. So you might say to yourself:

I fell off my horse today. I'm glad I wasn't injured, but it still hurt. I ache because of it. I'm really proud of myself for getting back on, even though I felt quite scared. It's shaken my confidence though and I feel a bit disheartened by it, which is only natural. I'm going to run a nice hot bath and have a soak to soothe my body. I think I'll reward myself with a glass of wine too, because I was very brave to get back on again! I did well today.

In this scenario, you have honoured the shock of the fall, acknowledged that it hurt and that it's knocked your confidence in your riding ability and come up with a plan to soothe the aches and pains, at the same time as giving yourself a small reward, with a glass of wine. Finally, you acknowledged your bravery and how well you dealt with the situation. This is self-soothing in action. It is a series of micro-acknowledgments and little steps that you take to make yourself feel better about any given situation. Here is another example.

Imagine that you are relaxing at home, reading a thrilling novel and the phone rings. When you answer it, the person on the other end immediately starts to berate you for something they think you did, or didn't do. They won't listen to your attempts to reason with them, instead they bring other people into the conversation at their end. Before you know it, you are in the midst of a full blown row over the phone, when all you were doing is sitting quietly at home, reading your book and minding your own business. How does self-soothing work in this instance? Again, you might have a mental conversation with yourself, such as:

I am being verbally attacked. They aren't listening to me at all. They are only interested in attacking me. I feel ambushed and pummelled.

*This is very unfair. I don't deserve this kind of treatment. But I don't
have to put up with it. I have a choice. I'm going to end the phone
call now, then I'll write in my journal until I feel calm again. I will
not speak to this person again unless they apologise for their attack. I
will start to screen all my calls to protect myself from this happening
again. I will record the time and date of their call in case I need to
make a formal report of it.*

Once again, you have acknowledged the event and the fact that
you have just been verbally attacked, ambushed while you were
simply minding your own business! You have validated your feeling
of being ambushed and decided to use journalling as a way to
process those feelings and get the negativity out of your system.
Finally, you have stepped into your body-guard persona by taking
back your power in ending the conversation, screening all future
calls and recording the details of the attack, should you need to
alert the police. In this case, your journal becomes your personal
confident and is an act of self-soothing, but all these small actions
come together to make a plan for your own peace of mind.

DEEPER HEALING: REGAINING MENTAL CLARITY

In both the examples above, mental clarity was regained in the
midst of discord, simply by going through the steps of an internal
conversation with yourself. This technique can be used in any
situation, whenever you feel under attack, out of control, or in a
state of minor shock. The steps are:

1. Acknowledge the event – what just happened?

2. Honour your emotions - how do you feel about it?

3. Validate those feelings by telling yourself its ok to feel this
    way

4. Come up with a couple of simple self-care tasks that will help you to feel better in the moment

5. Step into your power in some way – protect yourself

SELF-PARENTING

In essence, self-soothing is a form of self-parenting, which is when you treat yourself as a loving parent would treat a child who is hurt or upset. This is a very good skill to have, especially if your parents were emotionally distant or you had a difficult childhood. In self-parenting, you are offering yourself the loving care and attention that you perhaps missed out on in childhood.

Think about how a parent soothes a child after a fall, or through illness. They stroke their hair and forehead, hug them tight, rock them on their knee, run warm baths, wrap them in blankets or tuck them into bed, make delicious treats to eat, and warm drinks to sip. All of these are very simple acts of care and compassion, and when you give them to yourself, you are parenting yourself in a very nurturing and positive way. Below are some tips on things you can do to soothe and parent yourself.

-   Make your favourite hot drink from childhood, such as cocoa or warm milk

-   Make your favourite nursery food – rice pudding, soft boiled eggs and toasted soldiers to dip, porridge etc.

-   Wrap yourself in a soft, cosy blanket or scarf

-   Hug a hot water bottle in a fluffy cover

-   Put a weighted blanket on your bed, as this is designed to feel like a hug

- Wrap your arms around your waist and hug yourself

- Sit in a rocking chair or garden hammock – the rocking motion imitates the safety of being rocked in a parent's arms

- Have a long soak in a hot bath

- Use body lotion or massage oils – this imitates a parent putting talc or lotion on you as a baby

- Seek out things that make you laugh – watch funny animals on social media, or a comedy, or cartoons. Laughter is medicine.

- Plan a treat for yourself and book it in your diary.

FREE PLAY

Free play is a form of playfulness that is entirely self-directed. Psychotherapists use it as a technique to help people reconnect with their inner child and the freedom of doing things just for fun. In this way, the inner child's unmet needs often come to the surface, where self-parenting can then be used to meet those needs in adulthood. For instance, if you were often told off for playing too loudly as a child, then you might have difficulty expressing yourself in adulthood. In this case, part of the therapy would focus on you using your voice more, perhaps incorporating singing or laughter techniques, to help you end your silence and speak up.

Free play is one of the most fun aspects of self-care because you get to do all the things you might have been too busy to enjoy as an adult. Art, music, digging around in the garden, playing a sport, dancing, playing games, crafting and so on, can all be used as forms of free play. Try to incorporate some type of free play into your week, using the suggestions below to get you started.

- Colour in an art therapy colouring book

- Knit, crochet or sew something

- Make something from wood

- Paint a picture

- Start a jigsaw puzzle

- Plant a few flowers or herbs in the garden or window-box

- Feed the birds and see how many you can identify

- Ride a bike

- Play a sport

- Learn to play a musical instrument

- Attend a dance class

- Stretch and move to your favourite music

- Re-watch your favourite movies and cartoons from childhood

- Re-read the books you loved as a child

- Play with makeup

- Play dress-up and discover new ways to wear your old clothes

- Play games with your kids, or by yourself

- Have a movie marathon

- Go to the park or woods

- Schedule a Free Play day in your diary and do whatever you feel like on that day

- Take yourself on an adventure of some kind

WITCHY WAYS: MAGICAL BATHS

Soaking in a fragrant bubble bath or jumping under a hot shower is one of life's simple pleasures. There is nothing quite like sinking into the tub after a long day at work or stepping into the shower after playing a strenuous sport or following a challenging gym session. Water is a great healer and it is no accident that people going through hard times sometimes find themselves weeping in the shower or the bath, because water is the element of emotion.

Cleansing is obviously part of your basic care and hygiene routine, but it can be so much more than that, given a little extra thought. Magical baths are laced with intention, so you can bring about a sense of calm, deep healing, rejuvenation and so on, as you soak. If showers are more your thing, then simply take the ingredients of the magical baths and use them in the shower instead, adding essential oils to salt as a body scrub, or placing a couple of drops in the corner of the shower so the scent rises with the steam.

A Restorative Lavender Bath Potion

Items required: a voile pouch, muslin cloth or hankie, two teaspoons of dried lavender, one teaspoon of dried camomile flowers, a lavender ribbon, lavender essential oil.

Timing: use this spell whenever you are feeling particularly stressed but it works all the better on a full moon

Stress is a part of daily life and one that we must take steps to minimize and counteract. However, when you are feeling particularly stressed, you probably won't have the energy to work a full ritual. That's where bath potions come in. They can be made up in advance and kept in an air tight jar, ready for use when you need them most. For this restorative bath potion, you will need two parts dried lavender, mixed with one-part dried camomile flowers. Both these herbs are well known for their healing and restful properties. If there is a more restful way to de-stress than soaking in a fragrant lavender bath, I haven't found it yet! This is one of my staple remedies.

First make the bathroom enticing. Light candles if you want to and run a hot bath. Place the dried herbs into the pouch, or in the middle of the hankie and tie it tightly using the ribbon. As the bath fills, swirl the pouch of herbs in the water in a clockwise direction, scenting the hot water with fragrance. Imagine that once you sink into the water, all your cares will float away on lavender clouds. Tie the pouch to the tap so that it hangs in the water. As a final step, add ten drops of lavender essential oil to the water just before you sink into the depths. Relax and breath in the fragrance. Allow the herbal scent to calm you and let go of any stressful thoughts. Remain in the water for as long as you can, making the most of the restful energies of the herbs. When you are ready, dry off and empty the wet herbs into the earth, giving back what you have taken. Enjoy the remainder of your day and do calming, gentle activities to maintain your sense of peace. You can also use this pouch in a shower, hanging it by the shower head and letting the steam release the scents.

Anti-Fatigue Peppermint Bath

Items required: peppermint and eucalyptus essential oils, one lemon or lemon juice, fresh mint and eucalyptus leaves (optional)

Timing: prepare this bath whenever you are feeling fatigued and exhausted

Chronic fatigue can be incredibly debilitating. For some it is a long term illness, for others it is temporary and is a result of overwork or high levels of stress. This bath remedy is very simple, but remarkably effective. Peppermint is well known for its rejuvenating powers. The scent is very uplifting and invigorating, which helps to alleviate the fatigue. This bath remedy isn't a long term fix, but it can certainly help you to feel less tired and put a pep in your step. As you run a warm bath, add ten drops of peppermint essential oil and six drops of eucalyptus oil which will sooth tired limbs and aching muscles. Next you can either add in a tablespoon of lemon juice, or one fresh lemon sliced. This added zest will give your energy levels a boost. Add the fresh leaves if you have them just before you get into the water. Soak in the water for a while and allow the scents to invigorate you and ease away the fatigue. This is a very uplifting and stimulating bath, so probably one to enjoy during the morning, rather than at bedtime.

Eucalyptus Ritual for a Sacred Night-time Shower

Items required: a stem of fresh eucalyptus

Timing: in the evenings

Showering off the day before bed is a sacred time of self-care. It helps your mind to move from work time into home and family time and it can aid in a restful night's sleep. To give your bathroom a more magical spa-like atmosphere, hang a branch of fresh eucalyptus inside the shower, where the steam will release its calming scent. As you shower, imagine all the psychic grime of the day washing away from you and going down the drain. Breathe in the rejuvenating scent of eucalyptus and know that you are safe at home and it is time to switch off and relax. You can enhance this spell by using lavender or eucalyptus scented toiletries.

Pink Self-Love Bath Potion

Items required: pink candles, pink Himalayan salt, a few rose petals

Timing: perform whenever you are feeling frazzled

There will be days when you feel that you cannot do anything right, when you've been running late since the beginning and one mishap led straight into another, leaving you feeling stressed and decidedly frazzled. On those days, show yourself some love with this bath potion. Mix together equal parts pink Himalayan salt and rose petals, then stir this mixture into a hot bath. The salt is known to reduce fatigue, replacing tiredness with feelings of contentment and emotional balance, while the rose petals will soften the skin as the fragrance uplifts you. Wallow in the water for as long as you comfortably can, then dry off and allow your troubles to go down the drain, ensuring that you dispose of the rose petals on the compost heap. Enhance this ritual by using rose scented toiletries.

SIMPLE SELF-CARE: A GROUNDING CRYSTAL MEDITATION

Items required: two jade or green aventurine crystals

Timing: as the sun sets

At the end of a long day, use this grounding ritual to let all the stress and strain slip away. Wait until the sun begins to set, then sit on the floor in a comfortable position. If the weather is nice you can perform this ritual outdoors, if not do it inside. Breathe deeply several times until you begin to feel relaxed and centred. Next pick up the green crystals and hold one in each hand. Close your eyes and visualise any stress, anxiety or negative energy moving through your body, into the crystals, then out from the crystals and into the earth. See this stream of energy in your mind's eye and watch as the dark energy of your stress is neutralized by the crystals, turning a brilliant shade of emerald green, before it disappears into the earth. Allow the earth to absorb your stress, your worries, your anxiety, knowing that it will transform this energy into fresh growth and greenery. When you are ready, open your eyes. Give thanks to the earth and the crystals, run the crystals under cold water to cleanse them and go about your evening.

CHAPTER 9

WHAT DOESN'T KILL YOU

There is no doubt that some people have a more difficult life experience than others. In life, there is no level playing field and you have to learn how to play the game with the hand you've been dealt. Of course, it isn't fair that some individuals seem to have everything, while others have a lot less, but to a large degree, life is what you make of it. There will always be challenges along the way, no matter who you are. How you rise to meet those challenges is what separates those who are successful from those who are less so.

Resilience, robustness, inner strength – call it what you will, but make no mistake about it, it is a *learned response*. The school of hard knocks might be harsh at times, but it is also the fastest way to learn and to earn your stripes in resilience. It is during your most difficult times that you are being moved up to the next level of life and while you might not always achieve that level first time round, you are nonetheless acquiring skills and experience that will prepare you for the next stage of your life.

Inner strength *does* come more easily to some people, it's true, but even they have had to hone this skill. Robustness is very much something that is largely self-taught. If you have never been tested, then you have never had a chance to learn this skill. This is why being cosseted as a child actually works to your detriment in adulthood. Overly protective parents are often referred to as helicopter parents, because they constantly hover over their kids, always ready to catch them if they stumble, always available to fight their battles for them, never giving them a chance to grow up and develop their spirit of independence. This can continue well into adulthood. It is not just something that happens to young children. Helicopter parenting is toxic, because it means that the parent never gives the child a chance to fall or fail, meaning that they never learn how to get back up again. In short it robs the child of the chance to develop their resilience. This later presents itself in adulthood as incapability, frailty, neediness, anxiety and learned helplessness.

RESILIENCE VS. SNOWFLAKE CULTURE

We live in an age that allows people to live in a state of learned helplessness, to be hyper sensitive and easily offended by small things. We call it snowflake culture and it is the opposite of resilience. Snowflake personalities can be found in any age group, though it is the millennials who get all the bad press. When we talk about people being snowflakes, or flaky, we are referring to the fact that they lack confidence in their own abilities and they exist in a state of learned helplessness. In addition, with greater awareness of mental health conditions such as anxiety and depression, snowflake personalities often play the mental health card to get out of doing anything that makes them uncomfortable – which, because they exist in learned helplessness, is most things! Furthermore, society allows and even encourages this, under the diversity agenda. Obviously there are people who struggle more than others in their day to day life, but we should be gently nurturing their inner strength, rather than encouraging their continued incapacity and hyper sensitivity.

Resilience on the other hand is living from a state of capability and strength. It is knowing that you can cope with the events life presents to you, that you will manage somehow and come out the other side stronger than you were before the experience. While snowflake personalities buckle into a melt-down whenever life gets tough, resilient ones buckle-up and prepare for a bumpy ride ahead. They might not like it, but they have a sense of survival that gets them through it.

SIMPLE SELF-CARE: CHALLENGE YOURSELF

Becoming more resilient and robust is a decision that must be made by the individual. It cannot be forced. However, once that decision has been made it is simply a matter of challenging yourself and learning to get comfortable in uncomfortable situations. You are unlikely to become more robust if you never step outside of your comfort zone, or if you are constantly seeking out the nearest safe space. Life will frequently present you with challenges to overcome. You might lose a job or a lover, struggle with debt or suffer a bereavement. This doesn't mean that life is out to get you, it just means that you are being offered a lesson in the school of hard knocks. They might be unpleasant, but such events are an opportunity for you to become stronger.

You can also pre-empt these events by taking on less distressing challenges as part of your day to day life. Do something that stretches your feeling of safety – take a climbing class, learn to swim, drive somewhere you've never been before, run a marathon etc. In taking on every day challenges, you are quietly nurturing your inner strength and personal robustness, so that when the big challenges of life come along, such as deaths and disasters, you have already built up a bank of resilience to draw upon. The more you challenge yourself, day to day, the more robust you will become.

WITCHY WAYS: REQUEST A HAPPY CHALLENGE

This easy spell calls on the universe to send a happy kind of challenge your way. It could be that you are asked to give a presentation or take on more responsibility at work, or that you are asked to babysit, or to give a speech of some kind. It could also manifest as an opportunity to take part in a high adrenaline sport such as abseiling or sky-diving for charity. Whatever it is, it will be a chance for you to push yourself and challenge yourself in a safe way, so if you are ready to spread your wings a bit, cast this spell on the next new moon to bring challenging new opportunities your way. Take a tea-light candle and hold it close to your heart as you say the incantation below, then light it and allow it to burn down naturally. Your challenge should present itself within three lunar months.

I'm ready to leave my comfort zone

To spread my wings and fly

I'm ready to be challenged, new skills to hone

To give my inner strength a try

New opportunities come to me

I ask the universe to send

The right kind of challenge for me

So that I can begin to ascend.

So mote it be

WITCH, HEAL THYSELF!

There is a saying in Wicca, '*Witch, heal thyself first*', meaning that, we can be of no service to anyone else unless we are strong in mind, body and spirit ourselves. Helping other people to solve their problems is part of being a witch. Basically this means that witches help people to help themselves - we don't wave a magic wand and make all their problems go away for them, but we do encourage them to look at things from a different angle or offer a fresh perspective. But what happens when the witch herself falls ill? Well, then she must focus on self-healing and self-care, which is essentially what you are doing with this book.

When witches talk about healing they allude to the fact that they are working to bring about a state of balance and alignment. This is as true for healing the psyche as it is for healing the body. To a large extent, the body is self-healing, though it requires medical intervention from time to time. The mind is less so, however, and so restoring balance in the realm of mental health can take some time and effort. This is because you need to become aware of the imbalance before you can address it. In a nutshell, that is the purpose of this book – to help you begin to heal your deeper issues, the ones you might not even realize you had, but which were having a negative impact on your day to day life and sense of wellbeing. That is the heart of self-care – to become as mentally self-healing as you can possibly be.

Nurturing your robustness is a form of mental armour. It means that life's little niggles will have less of an impact on you, while bigger challenges you face will be overcome more easily. Robustness is what takes your mind from fear, to fierce in an instant. It is that sense of personal equilibrium when disaster strikes, or when the unexpected happens. When you have the balance of robustness you are unlikely to break down completely or lose your head in a crisis. It is a protective mental device for dealing with stressful situations.

Witches believe that people are never given more than they can cope with. You already have everything within you that you need to rise to challenges and to overcome hardship, you just need to tap into that inner resource. While the universal energies will undoubtedly stretch you, sometimes almost to breaking point, where you feel that you can't cope, you do have much deeper reserves of strength than you may know. Resilience and robustness are the channels through which this strength is utilized.

WITCHY WAYS: WITCH, HEAL THYSELF RITUAL

This is a good spell to use whenever you feel that you need a bit of extra help in coming to terms with your healing journey. The teachings of this book might have brought up some deep seated issues that you are struggling to confront. That's okay. You are not expected to heal old traumas overnight. You can work through the exercises of this book as many times as you need to, in order to address your old wounds. Mental healing can be a tough process, but it is worth the effort. This healing ritual will help to soothe you when it all gets a little too much, so show yourself some tender loving care by using this massage oil.

You will need lavender and ylang ylang essential oils, a carrier oil such as almond or olive oil and a dark glass mixer bottle. Pour 10mls of the carrier oil into the mixer bottle and add five drops each of the lavender and ylang ylang oils. Put on the lid and shake the bottle thoroughly to blend the oils together. Use this as a massage oil, rubbing it into your skin using long, even strokes, moving towards the heart to get the blood flowing. Inhale the healing aroma and say these words as you continue to massage in the fragrant oil.

I am worthy of healing

I am strong from within

I am healing old wounds

I feel the healing begin

I am releasing all toxins

I am strong to my core

I am worthy of healing

I am strong evermore.

DEEPER HEALING: PRODUCTIVE REST

When your body is in the process of healing, from the flu for example, you know that you need more rest. You curl up under the duvet and snooze the day away until you begin to feel better. Yet when people are healing mentally, they seem to imagine that they should continue as normal. This is often a recipe for burn out and back slides.

Mental healing takes a lot of energy. It can leave you feeling exhausted and fatigued. Just because you cannot see the healing process taking place, doesn't mean that your body isn't doing anything. Your mind is busy recalibrating itself, coming to terms with a new found awareness, perhaps regurgitating memories and flashbacks of things that you have repressed and which need to be addressed. It is working overtime, so cut yourself some slack and allow yourself more time to rest. If you are waking up tired, spending your days in a fog of fatigue and you feel constantly exhausted, then these are all signs that you are not getting enough rest and relaxation time.

Your body and mind heal best when you are well rested, but there is more to rest than falling asleep in front of the TV. Productive rest tends to be the most beneficial, as opposed to passive rest, and of course, deep, restorative sleep is essential to your wellbeing. Here are a few ways that you can get the rest you need in a beneficial and productive way.

- Write in your journal

- Read a book

- Arrange flowers

- Give yourself an aromatherapy massage (see above)

- Deep breathing exercises

- Sleep next to your pet

- •Allow yourself to fall asleep in a sunny space (but not in direct sunlight)

- Structure your time and plan your diary

- Lay down and listen to relaxing music

- Go for a gentle walk

- Spend time in nature, sitting with the trees

- Listen to the birds singing, or the waves coming into shore, or the wind in the trees

- Listen to a guided meditation

- Sleep when you need to and wake up naturally

WITCHY WAYS: BLESSING FOR SWEET DREAMS & RESTFUL SLEEP

Items required: lavender sleep spray

Timing: perform each time you change the bed sheets

For a deeper, more restful sleep, start to include this blessing as part of your household chores. First of all, change the bed sheets and as you put on the clean bedding, spray it generously with the lavender sleep spray, inside and out. Give every part of the bedding a spray, so that the fragrance envelops the sleeper when they get into bed. You can also use a lavender scented ironing water to the same effect. As you spritz the bed say the following incantation:

Lavender let the dreams be sweet

For all who lie within these sheets

I cast this spell with love and charm

To keep the sleeper safe from harm

So mote it be

As you finish making the bed pat the pillow three times saying, *Rest, Recharge, Restore.* Hang a dream catcher close by for additional good energy.

BOUNCE RIGHT BACK!

The secret to taking life in your stride is to constantly adjust and re-adjust your step. Bouncing back from hardship, conflict, danger and disaster is a matter of learning from the experience and then being able to let it go and move on. Holding onto the negative aspects of the event will only drag you down into negative thought spirals, anxiety, depression, feelings of failure and so on.

Bad things happen to good people all the time. It's just a fact of life, but that doesn't make it any easier when bad things are happening to *you*! Ignoring it doesn't work either, because when you bury your head in the sand the situation is likely to get worse, not better. Acknowledge that things haven't quite gone to plan. Then make a new plan to deal with the change in circumstances. Having resilience and robustness means that you will, quite naturally, develop a stronger bounce-back ability. This in turn means that you are less likely to take a set-back personally, or be derailed by it.

You can take steps to ensure that you bounce back more quickly by sifting through the events and looking at what you can and can't control. Make a list of all the things that are within your control and start to come up with a viable plan of action to move forward. At the same time, accept that there will always be things that are outside of your control. Knowing the difference between the two, means that you won't waste valuable time trying to change things over which you have no personal agency. Sometimes life throws a spanner in the works and no-one is at fault.

It is also a good idea to always have a Plan B ready. In this way, you are not putting all your eggs into one basket and should your initial plans go awry, you have an alternative to fall back on. You never know what is round the corner and there will undoubtedly be times when you will be glad to have a Plan B in your back pocket, just in case. Having a back-up plan like this means that you are thinking ahead, planning for a possible set-back and giving yourself an alternative route to follow instead. This prevents you from wallowing over the failed Plan A. Instead you can press ahead with Plan B and remain focused on moving forward and getting ahead. Even the military understand that no plan survives first contact with the enemy and that they will have to change course at some point.

DEEPER HEALING: BUILD YOUR BOUNCE-BACK ABILITY
Compartmentalizing life can help you to keep things in perspective, as it is unlikely that every area of your life will go downhill at the same time. There are ways that you can help to mitigate the impact of a personal disaster and one of them is by ensuring that you have a shield of positivity around you, in different life arenas, to support you when things get tough. This ring is made up of five points and they are as follows:

- *Social support* – make sure that you have a strong team of friends, colleagues and professionals available to you and that you are moving in the right circles, mixing with positive people, rather than toxic ones.

- *Emotional support* – ensure that you are in a good place emotionally, working through any issues and acting from a place of emotional intelligence. Get professional help if you need it.

- *Physical support* – you can't bounce back if you are not taking good care of yourself. Exercise, eat well, get enough rest, drink plenty of water. Do what you need to do to keep your body strong.

- *Family support* – talk to your family members about what you are experiencing. Be open and receptive to their ideas. Let them help you. Lean on them when you need to. Enjoy spending time with them and let the love flow between you.

- *Spiritual support* - get in touch with your spirituality and grow from it. Meditate, cast spells, perform rituals, pray, practice mindfulness, attend spiritual services and events. Know that you are pure spirit in bodily form and you are guided and protected on your path.

CHAPTER 10
RE-BOOT YOUR MIND

Your mind is the strongest weapon that you have. You have seen how your habits can have a strong impact on how you feel and your overall wellbeing. Robustness is essential to being able to successfully navigate life's challenges but it is only half the battle. Knowing how best to fill your time, set goals and stand up for yourself, are also key components to living a happy life. They are all aspects of caring for yourself, maintaining motivation, avoiding ruts and becoming more accomplished. Living with dignity and autonomy is the right of every human being. That dignity begins with having respect for yourself, your boundaries and your sense of direction in life.

NEUROPLASTICITY

The brain is constantly processing, filing and organizing information. It takes on board all of your experiences and categorizes them. It automatically recalls the past in order to help you in the present, or plan for the future. As you learn new skills and have different experiences, your brain creates new neural pathways, or short cuts, so that it can quickly retrieve that new information in the future. All of this means that the mind is not static. It is not set in stone, but is a malleable organ that we can tinker with and adjust. We call this malleability *neuroplasticity*. It is a kind of computer programming for the mind, meaning that when we change the type of information we are feeding our brain, we can change how the brain reacts in different situations. This is especially useful for people who have experienced trauma.

Imagine a person who survives a terrorist attack at a large venue or city centre. The neural pathway the brain makes for that event is probably that large venues are dangerous and a risk to life, leading the individual to experience panic attacks, flashbacks etc., whenever they are in a crowded place. This is the brain's way of trying to protect and defend. It is part of the survival system at work, and it is screaming *'Get out now, before you get killed!'*.

However, it means that the individual concerned cannot lead a normal life, and so the neural pathway needs to be reset. This is done by gradually learning to get comfortable in public spaces, starting small and working up to a larger venue, such as where the attack happened. Using exposure therapy in this way, the brain is being gently reset, so that it no longer associates danger and death with busy places.

We can use this technique in lots of different ways. Resetting your mind is essential to break a habit, quit smoking, stop drinking and replace harmful things with healthier, more positive habits. It's just a case of re-booting the neural pathways and sending them off in a different direction.

DEEPER HEALING: CHANGE YOUR ASSOCIATIONS

Is there something in your life that has been caused and is maintained by a negative neural pathway? Do you associate all dogs with being bitten, for example, or all motorways with a road traffic accident? Do you refuse to go past a particular place because something bad happened there? If so, then you are being influenced by a neural pathway that is out of date. It can be tough re-visiting the past, especially recounting unhappy events or visiting the scene of the crime as it were, but it is essential if you are to move on and let it go.

Changing your associations is a great way to begin re-booting your mind. To do this, call to mind the negative event, person or place and allow the usual emotions to come up. Then interrupt this emotional response by changing the association to a happy and harmless one. For instance, if you associate all dogs with being bitten, feel that initial fear and distrust towards them, then interrupt the thought process by visualising puppies playing happily and licking you in glee. No-one can be frightened of a puppy! Keep doing this regularly to reset the neural pathway, and eventually you will be able to walk past a fully grown dog without too much discomfort or fear, because you have changed your association of dogs. This technique works for any negative thought association, but the deeper the trauma, the longer it takes, so stick with it and don't give up.

BETWEEN A RUT AND A DARK PLACE

Not all slumps are due to traumatic events and, thankfully, not all low moods will lead you to rock bottom. Sometimes, you might just feel a bit stuck in a rut. We all get into a rut every now and then and it is not unusual. It is just part of the ups and downs of life. If every day were super-exciting and adventurous, you would soon burn out! You need down time for several reasons. It helps to replenish energy levels, offers space to gain mental clarity and recalibrates your emotional frequency, leading to a more balanced approach to life.

A rut can be a hint that you are nearing burn out too, especially if you are still feeling very tired, despite not doing much. In this case, the rut is acting as a safety net, catching you before you fall into a deep negative spiral. Being in a rut gives you a chance to live a fairly low energy life. This low energy phase could be a temporary hiatus, or it could be something that you need to adopt as your long term lifestyle, particularly if you have a chronic illness to contend with. Trying to live life at full speed with chronic illness or pain is a recipe for disaster! Listen to your body and slow down.

There are different kinds of ruts. You might be in a work rut, where all you seem to do is work and sleep, with no time for any fun. You could be in a relationship rut – either not feeling connected to your partner, or having been single for a long time. Or perhaps you are constantly attracting and dating the wrong people. Maybe your rut is more personal and you feel worthless or under-valued. Whatever kind of rut you might be in, forward planning via time structuring and goal setting, is always the way out.

SIMPLE SELF-CARE: SET SOME GOALS AND MAKE A PLAN
Having something to aim for is good for your sense of self-worth. It will give you a reason to get up each day, to make plans and take steps to carry them through. It will also give you a sense of accomplishment, which is good for you for several reasons. First of all, it offers a sense of purpose. When life has no purpose it can start to feel stale and futile. Secondly, having a goal that is measurable means that you can actually see the progress you are making, and thirdly, it fosters the life-skills of persistence and determination.

To get out of a rut, change up your routine and do things differently. Set yourself a small, but meaningful goal, with a time frame in which you plan to achieve it. Then make a plan for *how* you will achieve it. Say your goal is to learn a musical instrument. You could begin by looking up classes in your area and booking in for a lesson. Then you might decide to download some easy sheet music for your chosen instrument. You might go shopping for your own instrument, or look into borrowing one. Next you could factor in daily practice and set time aside each day for your music, structuring your time around this commitment to your goal. As you move through the steps of this plan, you are gradually easing your way out of the rut and into a new dynamic phase of learning, expanding your life experience as you go and leaving the rut behind.

BEWARE OF APATHY

Apathy seems to be a modern epidemic. Far too many people are unhappy with their lot in life, yet unwilling to do anything about it. They are waiting for outside forces to change their life for the better - that jackpot lottery win, for instance, or the perfect partner to sweep them off their feet and into a life of luxury. While it *could* happen, it's not very likely, and you would be far better off, taking charge of your own life, rather than sitting around waiting for something or someone to do it for you.

Apathy, meaning a state of indifference, is passive by nature and psychotherapists see it all the time. People *want* to feel better but they are waiting for someone else to do all the hard work for them. The problem is that it is impossible to help someone who simply cannot be bothered with their own life. If you can't be bothered with your life, why would anybody else be bothered with it, or with you for that matter?

Apathy is exhausting. It makes you feel drained and leaves you in a state of daily inertia - doing nothing, sleeping too much, complaining often. Not only is it self-destructive, it can destroy your relationships too. Loved ones get tired of it, friends start to avoid you. Apathy's main partner is crime is excuse. Apathetic people will find any number of excuses not to change their life and to maintain their inertia. They're too sick, too tired, too depressed. They don't have the time, the money or the education. But the only way they will feel better is if they move out of a state of apathy and get pro-active instead.

SIMPLE SELF-CARE: WATCH YOUR EXCUSES!
How many excuses do you make for the way you live your life? Chances are, the more excuses you come up with, the more apathetic you are being. Are you waiting for circumstances to be just right before you make a move towards your goals? Are you telling yourself that you don't have the right background or

economic status to achieve success? Make a list of all the excuses you have used in the past week or so. What aspect of your life do these excuses relate to? Are you avoiding social settings for instance, because you lack confidence? Are you finding excuses not to go to work because you really hate your job and can't face going in? The excuses people make are often a very telling sign as to what is really going on in their psyche. What do your excuses say about you? What can you do to make positive changes in this area?

PERSONAL REINVENTION

Reinvention is a process of empowerment. If you are feeling stuck and like you're not getting anywhere, then changing how you think about yourself, how you see yourself, will have a positive effect on what you do and how you act. This in turn changes how others see you and in time, you can turn things around completely.

The happiest people seem to be the ones who like a challenge - those individuals who have ambition, set goals and do what they need to do to achieve them. Then they set new challenges and fresh goals. This creates the cycle of achievement, wherein achievement builds capability and capability builds personal confidence, so you feel able to take on bigger challenges. That is the secret to success.

Sometimes reinvention is subtle. Like a caterpillar in a chrysalis it may seem as if you are not doing much, but slowly the reinvention is taking place beneath the surface, away from prying eyes. This type of reinvention usually begins with boredom - you might be bored of doing the same job and feel the need to try something new. This might mean switching to a new arena within the same company, or trying for a promotion, or setting up your own business. Life is too short to stagnate! All you really have to do is to choose to be something else and then start moving in that direction instead.

Do what you need to do to move towards your goal - dress the part, act the part, speak the part and then one day, hey presto! - you are *living* the part and you have moved your life forward. At first it might feel as if you are wearing a mask or pretending to be something you're not. You might even have to deal with such comments from other people, but all you're really doing is listening to the whispers of your soul, which is asking you to grow into the person you have the potential to become.

Reinvention takes time, it isn't easy and it can be difficult, even painful at times, but know that you *are* capable of becoming a better version of yourself. Then go out and charm the world!

BECOME MORE ASSERTIVE

There is little point in doing all this self-care and psychological work on your mind-set, if you are going to buckle at the knees at the first hint of any conflict! Conflict is a fact of life, so the sooner you get comfortable confronting it, the better your life will be and the stronger you will become. Avoiding conflict means that you will never learn valuable skills such as standing up for yourself, recognising manipulation and assessing risk.

Assertiveness is not the same as picking fights. It is about standing your ground when someone is being confrontational. It means walking tall and not looking like an easy target when you're out and about. It is about learning to say no, asking for what you want and being self-assured. Perhaps most importantly, it is about knowing what victory looks like to you, so that you will recognise when you have won, rather than continuing to engage needlessly.

PLAYING SOLDIERS

Life can be a battle sometimes, so when you find yourself in the midst of a skirmish, you need to think like a soldier. Any busy road or workplace can quickly turn into a battlefield when tempers fray. While it's not a life and death situation, it can help to know exactly where you stand, by making a quick risk assessment. Your back up might be your boss, your safety zone your desk, your communication device your mobile phone etc. Thinking like a soldier will help you to remain calm and collected, and less likely to lose your temper in retaliation. You can command a difficult situation with an air of capability and quiet authority simply by maintaining self-control and an assertive demeanour.

SIMPLE SELF-CARE: CONDUCT A RISK ASSESSMENT
When faced with any kind of confrontation, assess the situation as a soldier would, by asking yourself the following questions.

- Are you in any immediate danger?

- Is this territory yours, theirs or neutral ground?

- Have you been ambushed or taken by surprise (e.g.. road   rage)?

- Are you out-numbered?

- Do you have back-up?

- Are your communication devices working?

- How far are you from safety?

An assessment like this will give you the information you need to know, so that you can decide what your next move should be. It could be that you call for back up, or that you leave the situation and move on. It could be that you are not under threat, but you have stumbled into a chaotic incident or accident of some kind and you have the skills to intervene and help. But you won't know until you have done the risk assessment, because as they say, knowledge is power.

DEEPER HEALING: MANIPULATION - KNOW THE SIGNS!
Manipulation and coercion are easy enough to spot when you know the signs to look out for. If someone is trying to manipulate you they are likely to turn on the charm offensive, cajoling and flattering you into doing what *they* want, rather than what you want. Here are the signs that someone is trying to manipulate you:

- **Suspicion** - if you feel suspicious, this is your intuition telling you to beware, because chances are, this person doesn't have your best interests at heart.

- **Confusion** - feeling befuddled, or someone leading the conversation round in circles to deliberately confuse you, is a sure sign that you are dealing with a manipulative character.

- **The Bind** – they try to put you in a bind by offering you a false choice between two things, both of which they know you don't want. In this situation you should always take the third option, which is the one they fail to mention – go your own way and choose something else entirely that you do want! So if they are offering you a choice between spinach or sprouts, choose the chocolate cake instead!

- **Assumed Negative** - they say things like "You don't mind if I...do you" and "You haven't got a problem with...have you?" They are making the assumption that you will say no and so fall in line with their plans. Don't fall for it. Say "Actually, yes I do mind."

- **Disregard** - manipulative people will try to disregard your refusals. They don't hear the word No and they try to make you feel like you are the one who is being unreasonable. Try saying "You disregard everything I say, so I see no point in continuing this discussion. You've had my answer. I said no." and walk away.

- **Questioning Trust** - if you find yourself asking "Can I trust this person" it is a sign from your intuition that you don't trust them, whereas a manipulative character will ask "Don't you trust me?" in order to get under your defences and force trust. Listen to your instincts and trust those instead.

SIMPLE SELF-CARE: DON'T BE A DOORMAT!

Are you tired of being put upon by friends or undermined at work because you are too nice for your own good? Do you frequently find yourself saying yes to favours when you'd much rather say no? If you are the go-to person for a favour, it could be damaging your mental health. Giving too much of your time and support to others can lead to compassion fatigue which leaves you feeling drained and fed-up. It also means that your friends will expect more from you, simply because you're always ready to help out, making you feel used and under-appreciated. The best way to avoid being taken for granted is to be very selective with your favours. You shouldn't have to justify a refusal. Say no firmly, without giving a list of reasons or apologies. "*No.*" is a complete sentence in itself. Say it once and don't back down. In this way you are retraining your friends to accept that your refusal is final.

WITCHY WAYS: LIPSTICK AFFIRMATIONS

Using the same lipstick or lip balm each time, say one or two of the affirmations below, apply the lipstick and then repeat the affirmations again. Subsequently, each time you reach for the lipstick and apply it, repeat the affirmations.

I am strong and resilient

I speak with the tone of command

I see my own capability

I assert my right to say NO

I refuse to be manipulated by anyone

I think like a soldier, calmly and self-possessed

WITCHY WAYS: BE YOUR OWN BOSS RITUAL

You are meant to be the boss of your own life and no-one else has the right to try and take that job away from you. Even in the workplace, providing that you are carrying out your duties and responsibilities with all due diligence, you shouldn't regard anyone else as being the boss of you. They might be in a higher rank or a managerial position, but they are not in charge of your autonomy, you are. Self-agency is vital in building confidence and esteem, yet manipulative characters will often chip away at your autonomy because it makes you easier to manipulate. Don't stand for it. Cast this spell on a daily basis to safe-guard your autonomy. Every morning, dip your finger into a little moisturiser and use it to paint the Algiz rune over your heart and your third eye. This is the protective rune of the warrior and it will act as a type of psychic shield. As you draw on the rune say the following words, then rub the rune into your skin.

I wake up strong, I suffer no fools

I'm no puppet on a string

I'm the boss of me, I make the rules

I have autonomy in all things

So mote it be.

CHAPTER 11

BLUE SKIES

The battleground of life is much easier to navigate if you can identify where the psychological landmines are likely to be and then take steps to avoid them, or at least mitigate their impact. Keeping an eye on areas of potential conflict in your life and recognising possible triggers for psychological wounds is essential if you don't want to be ambushed by negative contact, unexpected events and haunting shadows from your past.

We are all deeply influenced by the events of our past, just as much as those in our present. Some life events are unavoidable: others will give you a head's up that they are on way so that you can prepare for them in advance. Bereavement is unavoidable, for instance, and everyone experiences it at some stage. Divorce on the other hand, rarely comes as a completely unexpected surprise and there are usually signs along the way that the relationship is crumbling.

Obviously some events can quickly tip you into a negative life spiral, which is exactly what we want you to avoid! There will always be certain areas of your life that are less stable than others. Maybe your job is secure but your marriage is rocky, or vice versa. Bearing in mind what we looked at earlier in the book, about one negative event leading to another, it is important that you learn how to recognise potential flashpoints so that you can do some damage limitation, in advance of the event. In this chapter then, we are going to explore some of the most common circumstantial changes which can trigger a downward spiral and ways of lessening their negative impact on your wellbeing.

LOSS AND SADNESS

Loss is part of life, from the big life-changing losses, such as losing a job or a limb, to the smaller everyday losses, like losing your purse or your credit card, every kind of loss can have a negative impact on you. It must be said too, that sometimes you might lose something because it is not serving you, or it is not in your best interests. However, this doesn't make the impact of the loss any easier to endure. A missed opportunity can still leave you feeling pretty low, until something even better comes along, which it usually does, given time.

Depression and low mood are a natural consequence of deep sadness, so when you lose something, or someone, that means a lot to you, a dip in the scales of your emotional balance is inevitable. The deeper the sadness and the more final the loss, the bigger the dip in your mood and the harder it is to recalibrate your emotional balance and sense of equilibrium. This is quite normal, but it can be very difficult to actually live through.

However, there is always something you can do to find the silver lining and to feel better about the event. Even death has something to teach us, though this is the harshest lesson in the school of hard knocks. Let's take a look at common ways in which your life could change for the worse and explore how to make it better.

BEREAVEMENT

Death is the only guarantee that life has to offer, meaning that bereavement is inevitable. At some stage in your life, someone you love will die and you will feel left behind. For most people, this is their darkest hour. A bereavement impacts all aspects of your life – work, relationships, family dynamics, physical and mental health, finances, sense of belonging etc. No stone is left unturned when a loved one dies, for death touches everything. You will be raw with grief and loss, wondering how you will go on without that person in your life.

This is all the worse, if the person who has died is the one you used to turn to for help. Usually, this role is taken by a much loved parent, but not always. It could be your spouse or an older sibling. Losing our main care-giver from childhood is especially wrenching, as is losing your life partner. It can leave your feeling completely unmoored and out of kilter. It can mean that you lose your moral centre and begin to participate in risky behaviour, such as promiscuity or experimenting with drugs to numb the pain. This is when the secondary level of trauma, such as abuse and addiction can kick in, meaning you now have two things to deal with, instead of one.

What happens when you lose someone you didn't get along with, someone you love to hate? Is this any easier to cope with? In a word, no. Losing a difficult parent, spouse or sibling can be quite devastating, because not only does the grief take you by surprise, but it carries with it the knowledge that now, all hope is lost, and that person will never be the kind of companion and support you always hoped they would be. This double whammy of finality can be excruciating and its impact should never be underestimated.

DEEPER HEALING: COPING WITH BEREAVEMENT

It takes time to comes to terms with the death of a loved one. Often the real loss only hits you six to twelve months after the death itself, as initially you are protected by a sense of numbness. This is also the time when all the support that was initially offered has trickled away, as people return to their own lives, leaving you isolated in your grief. Professional grief counselling can help and so can keeping the event in perspective, because as hard as it is to accept, death is a natural part of life. Here are some tips for coping with its aftermath.

- Remember that death is not personal. It simply is.

- Talk about the person who died. Keeping their memory alive is very healing.

- Talk *to* the person who died, either out loud or in your head. Keep them informed about your triumphs and accomplishments, low, sad days and funny mistakes.

- Write a letter to the person who died and tell them exactly how you feel. If you are full of anger towards them, write it all down and tell them why. Burn the letter, but don't be afraid to repeat this process as often as you need to. Anger at the deceased is not uncommon and it doesn't mean you love them any less. You're just angry that they left you, or were never there for you in life.

- Plant something in their memory. This will remind you that life goes on and you will gain pleasure in seeing it grow, mature and change as it evolves through the seasons.

- Try not to wallow too much on the anniversary of the death. Celebrate their life in some way instead.

- Bereavement takes its toll on your physical and mental health, so take extra care of yourself and maintain a good routine of self-care tasks. At least make sure that you are hitting those Survival Level tasks each day.

LOSS OF A RELATIONSHIP

The ending of a relationship is very similar to a bereavement, in that you have to go through a grieving process. Often there are signs that the relationship isn't working and you might have been turning a blind eye to these signs in the hopes that the problems will go away or somehow resolve themselves.

Sometimes the end of a relationship comes out of the blue, with no warning whatsoever. You might come home from work early to find your partner in bed with someone else, for example, or discover that they have been having an affair for years. Infidelity is a common cause of divorce or breakup and the sense of betrayal can be acute.

Even if your relationship has quietly deteriorated over a number of years, it can still be hard to let it go. You might feel unhappy, but are unable to make the break. This is especially true if you have a Try Hard psychological driver. It could also be that it is your partner who wants to break it off and you feel somewhat blind-sided by this turn of events.

Whatever the reason for the split, you haven't only lost your lover, but the familiar routines of daily life and the future that you imagined with them too, possibly even your sense of identity. This might not be so bad if you are the one who is moving onto something or someone else, but if you're the one that has been dumped and left behind, it can be hard to process your new reality. Although in general, it is better to let go of a broken relationship and move on, that is easier said than done, however the following tips can help you to get through a breakup with your dignity intact.

- Don't beg them to stay. Keep your dignity, hold your head high and let them go. It's their loss.

- Don't weaponize the kids in order to get pay back on your spouse. This is unfair on the children and won't resolve anything.

- Don't stalk your ex on social media. Unfollow or mute them instead, or at least stop checking their feed.

- If you were the one to initiate the breakup, allow time for your ex to accept it really is over. This won't happen overnight. Understand that there are bound to be tears and tantrums, anger and expressions of betrayal.

- Don't give in to emotional blackmail. If you've made your decision, stick with it.

- Don't engage in any flirtatious or sexual behaviour in the post-breakup period. This is cruel and confusing.

- Don't be cruel, whatever side of the breakup you are on.

- Respect your ex-partner and be as gracious as you can be.

DEEPER HEALING: MAKE AN INFORMED DECISION

If you are in an unhappy relationship and you are considering breaking it off, allow yourself the time to make an informed decision. Don't act in haste after an argument or storm out by way of retaliation for something your partner did or didn't do. Wait at least 24 hours after the disagreement, then find a quiet place and write out a pros and cons list. What are the benefits of the relationship that you are currently in? What are the downsides? Does your partner make you cry more often then they make you laugh? Do you still have things in common? Are there more arguments and conflict than there are loving, harmonious interactions together? Be as objective as possible and write down as much as you can, covering all aspects of the relationship, from your sex life, to parenting, mutual support and domestic chores. Write it all down on paper, where you cannot hide from the facts.

Once you have your list, it should be easier to identify whether this relationship is contributing to your wellbeing, or costing you in some way. If there are more pros than cons, it could just be a case of tweaking the relationships until it fits you both better, say by attending couples counselling. However, if there are more cons than pros, then it might be time to part ways, but before you have that conversation, figure out what you would be losing and how you can replace those losses, without your partner. Once you have all the information in front of you, it will be easier to decide whether to stay or go.

LOSS OF HEALTH

Illness of any kind is the manifestation of the loss of health. It could be temporary, long term or terminal, but it will always have a negative impact on your life. Living with chronic pain or a long-term condition can be very debilitating, while receiving a terminal diagnosis, either for yourself or a loved one, can be completely devastating.

Healing can only go so far and there are some conditions that simply cannot be cured. Accepting the diagnosis can be difficult, as you come to terms with how it will change your life and affect your family members. Illness always has a ripple effect, so your loved ones will be just as affected by your illness as you are, although in an indirect way.

DEEPER HEALING: COPING WITH ILLNESS

Helping someone to navigate a healing journey that might involve operations, chemotherapy and recovery time, can be very stressful. Whether you are nursing someone, or you are the one who is sick, coming to terms with a loss of health is no easy task, but there are ways to lessen the blow.

- Accept that there are things that you can no longer do, sports you can't play, mountains you can't climb. Some aspects of your life will now be a part of your past.

- Try to incorporate joy into your life. Make a list of fun things to do and work your way through them with your family members.

- Spend time in nature and soak up her healing, energizing vibrations.

- Schedule mini-recovery days into your diary. This is essential if you are living with a long term illness such as chronic fatigue. If you know you have a busy day coming up, or a round of chemotherapy, schedule the following day in as recovery time so that you can get the rest you need.

- Adopt bed-friendly hobbies that you can do as you recover – needlework, blogging, colouring-in art therapy, crossword puzzles, reading etc.

- Live in the moment and do what you want to do, whatever makes you happy.

- Remember that recuperation takes time. You are trying to coax your health back to life and this kind of transformation requires rest and relaxation.

- Make your recuperation as pleasant as possible. Wear your nicest pyjamas, put on a face mask if you feel up to it, play beautiful music, listen to audio books or spoken word poetry albums, scent your bedding and pillows with a fragrant sleep spray. Lay back and let your loved ones bring you flowers and fruit and all good things!

LOSING A JOB

You spend over 84,000 hours of your lifetime working, so it should come as no surprise that many people build their sense of identity around what they do for a living. For most people, work is one of the things that makes us who we are, so when things go pear-shaped, it can spell disaster, in more ways than one.

Your job is how you survive in the world, giving you an income that pays for basic necessities such as food and shelter, so if you lose your job, you lose all sense of security too. This is further compounded if there are other people depending on you and your income for their survival as well, for instance a non-working spouse, children or elderly relatives.

Being told by an employer that your services are no longer required, for whatever reason, can feel like being run over by a steam roller, leaving you completely flattened by the news. Often this news comes out of the blue, or it might confirm your worst fears if redundancies have been on the cards. With the job also goes your sense of purpose, your income and security, even your identity. If you have lost a job you really love, you can add heartbreak to the list of woes too, as many people have a deep emotional attachment to their work. So much loss, all from the impact of losing a job. It's not surprising that job loss is one of the leading causes of a downward life spiral.

DEEPER HEALING: OPPORTUNITY IN REDUNDANCY
It can be hard to see any opportunity at all when you have just lost your job, but what you have actually been left with is a clean slate. You can use that slate to make plans for your future. Could you freelance in the same sector and become self-employed, still doing what you love, but in a more autonomous way? Could you use this space between jobs to re-train and upskill yourself? Could you start your own business? At the very least you have the chance to update your CV and make it as positive as possible. Could you

use this period of unemployment to write that book you've been dreaming of, or to become a content creator? What did you used to dream of doing during a bad day at your old job: what was your childhood ambition: could you take steps to achieve that dream now? Learn to see the silver lining and take it from there.

DEEPER HEALING: STEALTH ATTACKS
Sometimes it is trauma from the past which sneaks up on you when you least expect it, derailing your positivity and tipping you into a negative spiral. You might not even be able to pinpoint *why* you're feeling sad and low: you just know that you feel very down all of a sudden. The reason for this could be something that I call *stealth attacks* – that is, when an event from the past impacts your mood in a negative way in the present moment. Stealth attacks are caused by the mind associating a particular season, place or date with a traumatic episode. It is sometimes referred to as *the anniversary effect*. It acts like a psychological ambush, which leads to an emotional hangover. There are many instances which can cause this. These are some of the potential triggers to watch out for.

- *Birthdays and Death days* – the anniversary of a loved one's death, or the birthday of the deceased can have a negative impact on your wellbeing. This usually passes along with the date.

- *Dates and Hours* – this is the anniversary effect at play, when the date of a traumatic event rolls round year after year. It could be the wedding-date to your now ex-husband, the date you were attacked or were a victim of crime, the last time your spoke to a loved one before they passed away etc. The anniversary effect is powerful, so go easy on yourself at this time.

- *Dreams and Flashbacks* – this is when your trauma plays out in your mind, without your consent or control, which can be very disconcerting and disorienting.

- *Places* – Suddenly finding yourself in the same place where a traumatic event happened, or even somewhere that reminds you of that place, can be a huge trigger.

- *Seasonal Attacks* – Christmas is an obvious one, as it can carry a weighty emotional hangover for a lot of people. Other seasonal attacks could come with the summer holidays, springtime or a new school year.

- *Sounds and Smells* – these can come out of nowhere, at any time as you simply go about your day. They include smells reminiscent of an attacker's aftershave or sweat, the scent of the kind of flowers a stalker used to send, an old song that brings back bad memories etc. The sound of fireworks going off is a common trigger for veterans. The smell of tobacco might be a trigger for someone who was abused by a heavy smoker.

- *Taste* - tasting something that reminds you of past trauma.

- *TV* – suddenly seeing repeated news footage of past wars and hostile events, such as terrorist attacks you might have been caught up in, or where someone you know died, can catapult you into a low mood.

It can sometimes seem as if triggers are everywhere, but the more you learn to identify the potential for them, the better you will be able to protect yourself, either by avoiding them if the trauma is recent, or gently exposing yourself to them more and more, while in the company of a trusted friend. In the meantime, you can use the Self-Soothing methods from chapter 8.

THE POWER OF OPTING OUT

From a young age we are conditioned to believe that when the going gets tough, the tough get going. This is true to a certain extent and robust characters do tend to rise up to a challenge. However, there are times when it is more beneficial for you to just opt out of the fray. If you have experienced a period of frailty or illness, forcing yourself to keep going at a normal pace just isn't sustainable and in the long term, it could actually be harmful. Sometimes you need to give yourself permission to just opt out, skip an event, refuse an invitation and spend the day in bed with a book, or watching movies instead.

Christmas is an obvious example, as there is so much expectation surrounding this annual event, it can be difficult not to get caught up in the whirl of parties and social obligations. If you have just experienced a break up, a break down or a trauma of some kind, you are not going to feel like partying. Take back control and exert your right to opt out of anything that seems like it will be too much for you at this time. There will be other opportunities that come along when you are more ready to enjoy them.

CHAPTER 12

IN FOR A PENNY

Financial fear and money trauma are very real things. Money troubles are a big cause of stress, with debt charities being inundated with requests for help and doctors frequently asked for referrals to specialist counselling services, to help people deal with financial strain. Looking after your money is one of those areas of self-care that is often overlooked, as on the surface, it seems completely unrelated. Granted, money management isn't something you will find at a health spa, but as you have seen from this book, a large aspect of self-care lies in maintaining a degree of mental balance and money troubles can upset that balance quite easily. Here, we will look at ways you can improve your financial wellbeing.

FINANCIAL INTELLIGENCE

Developing financial intelligence is a type of transformative self-care, because your income is essential for you to live well and pay for the basics. Learning how to manage and take care of your money, means that you will have that sense of security which comes from earning more than you spend, and trusting that you will always have a certain level of income. This isn't about being filthy rich, or living an extravagant lifestyle, such as the ones displayed on social media. No, it is about generating an income which pays for all your needs and a few of your wants, with enough left over to build a healthy savings account for emergencies.

Financial intelligence involves making considered purchases, rather than impulsive ones. It means setting money aside to pay your taxes, if you are self-employed, so that there are no nasty surprises when your tax bill comes in. It is about knowing how much money you have in the bank, how much your monthly expenses are and what you can and can't afford. It means knowing where your spending triggers are and being able to identify when you have been influenced to spend money in a frivolous way. Little rewards are fine, but using credit to try and keep up with the Kardashians, or whoever, is not!

All aspects of basic financial intelligence are within your grasp. You don't need a degree in accounting or economics, you just need to have a firm grip on your own money, to know where it is going and how much you have left over at the end of the month. If there is more month than money, then you're in trouble and in the red! But if there's more money than month, you're in the black, so you can work on building your personal security blanket of wealth.

THERE IS NO WHITE KNIGHT

No-one is coming to rescue you financially. There is no white knight, charging in who will pay off all your debts and sweep you away to his castle in the air and a life of luxury that you don't have to work for. It isn't going to happen. What is far more likely, is that you will over-spend, ignore your debts and dig yourself into a much deeper financial hole, while you wait for him!

Pipe-dreaming is a common indicator that someone has stuck their head in the sand because they don't want to face the issue. Examples of financial pipe-dreams include a rich new partner coming to the rescue, or a lottery win, or a big gambling pay-off. Other more insidious indicators are saying things like '*Oh, if I just buy this extra special treat, then I'll feel more rich*' or '*I'll just buy this one last thing and then I'll start to save my money*'. The problem here is that you are constantly putting off addressing the issue and making financial intelligence a future task. It isn't. It is a task that you must practice daily, beginning today, especially if you want to become an expert on handling your own money effectively.

SIMPLE SELF-CARE: DEVELOP FINANCIAL INTELLIGENCE
The first step to financial intelligence is knowing exactly how much money you have coming in each month, how much your living expenses are, how much debt you are carrying etc. Learning how to hold onto your money is also a key factor in mastering your personal wealth.

- Work out how much your monthly income is, after tax. What is your take home pay? If you have multiple jobs or income streams, add them all together to get a single sum.

- Now work out how much all your living expenses are each month, including mortgage/rent, energy, phone, water rates, TV license, car expenses/public transport costs, groceries, pets, insurance costs. Add all these expenses together, to give you a single sum. (Automate them if you can, using direct debits and standing orders.) This is how much it costs you to live and cover the basics each month. It is your bottom line, your budget, your survival money.

- Next work out how much debt you have. If you can't face the sum total right now, just add up how much you need to pay each month i.e. the minimum payments each creditor requires. This is the minimum amount of money you need, to keep on top of your debts and avoid any additional costs and missed payment fees. It's your *keep out of trouble* money! (Again, automate these payments if you can, even if it's just the minimum payments due).

- Now add together your basic living expenses and your debt repayment expenses, to give you a single sum. This amount is your total monthly expenses. Subtract this sum from your total income and you will have a clear picture of whether you are living in the black or the red each month.

This can be a difficult exercise to complete, especially if you have been avoiding the issue of your finances for some time, but it is essential to know exactly where you are with your money. Remember that knowledge is power. It could be that you are not earning enough money to pay for everything, in which case, how could you generate more income? Could you ask for a pay rise, work overtime, get a better job, babysit, or start a side hustle? Is there a benefit you might be entitled to claim to boost your income? Conversely, this exercise could prove that you are making plenty of money to cover all your bills, with money to spare, but you still struggle at the end of each month. If that's the case, then it is likely that you are over-spending, so move on to the next exercise.

ARE YOU BEING INFLUENCED TO OVER-SPEND?

Money is a highly emotive issue. This is because we equate it with life and death. Having enough money to meet your basic expenses ensures your survival, while the opposite leads to hardship. In the past, not managing your finances correctly could get you thrown into a debtor's prison, so there is a historical residue attached to poor money management too.

Spending money is also very emotive, in that you feel a psychological high when you spend money on the things you want, the things that make your heart soar as you imagine the kind of person you will become, just as soon as you own a particular car, buy your dream house, or a horse, or even just that high-end lipstick you've been coveting.

Buying aspiration has never been easier than it is today. We even have an entire industry that is designed to profit from encouraging you to spend your hard earned money on things you don't need, often with just one click of a mouse. We call it the Influencer industry and it is worth billions of pounds. Understanding when you have been influenced to spend is key to holding onto more of your money. Knowing where your personal triggers are, is essential so that you can anticipate the influence and take steps to avoid acting on it. Magazines, shopping websites, social media platforms and advertisements, plus the Influencer industry, all conspire to make you part with your cash. Make a stand against these triggers, so that you can hold onto more of your income.

DEEPER HEALING: FIND YOUR TRIGGERS AND DRAINS

Where are you most inclined to spend money frivolously? Is it after visiting a friend who earns more than you and you want to emulate her home, her style and her life? Is it after watching a particular Influencer whom you admire, or a specific shop? What are your main weaknesses – books, clothes, perfumes, fancy bottles of wine, technology, cosmetics, travel? What makes your heart race at the thought of a purchase? How do you spend – is it online in the wee small hours when you can't sleep, at the weekends when you're out with friends, to cheer yourself up when you feel down in the dumps, or something else? Identifying these personal triggers mean that you can locate where your money drains are and block them. Learn to understand when someone is trying to sell your something and pause before you purchase. Do you really need it, or are you simply acting under the Influence? Do you own something similar already that could give you the same buzz if you used it or wore it more often? Can you borrow the item from a friend or relative and try before you buy? Finally block the drains by:

- Unsubscribing from triggering influences and Influencers

- Block newsletters and promotional emails

- Request to be removed from mailing lists

- Mark junk mail as Unaccepted - Return to Sender and put it back in the post. Repeat until they stop!

- Step away from the computer or leave the shop if you feel triggered to buy, buy, buy! Do something else instead.

- Delete shopping apps from your phone

- Understand that websites will claim to have very little stock left, of the items in your basket, in order to trigger your FOMO response – that is, your fear of missing out. Don't fall for it.

- Use the Pattern Interrupt technique to help your break bad shopping habits.

WITCHY WAYS: TEA OF PLENTY SPELL TO EASE MONEY WORRIES

Items required: a cup of peppermint tea

Timing: use this spell whenever you feel anxious about money

Peppermint is the herb of plenty, strongly associated with abundance and prosperity. Make a cup of peppermint tea in your favourite teacup or mug. Find a quiet place and sit with the tea. Breath in the scent of mint and try to calm your money worries. Think back to times when you were just as worried about making ends meet as you are now, but you made it through. Know that you will find a way to get through any lean times you might experience and trust that something will always turn up to help you. Imagine paying all your bills easily and having plenty of food to eat. Feel an emotion of plenty filling you as you sip the peppermint tea and take its gifts of prosperity into yourself. You and the mint are one, it fills you with abundance and hope. It warms you through with its comforting heat, it refreshes you for the time ahead. When you are finished with the tea, scatter the mint leaves in a garden or potted plant and give it back to the earth, with thanks.

SIMPLE SELF-CARE: SPENDING TRACKER

Becoming more financially intelligent involves tracking your spending. You now know how much your essential expenses are, but how often are you spending more frivolously? Using a spending tracker is a good way to see at a glance what your shopping habits are. There are many different spending trackers available, from printable downloads and apps to basic notebooks. Or you could make your own. Any will do, but getting into the habit of tracking your spending will help you to feel more in control of your money. Simply mark down each day whether you made any uncalled for purchases or not. Bear in mind, that companies spend millions of pounds trying to persuade you to buy their products and there is a deep level of psychology at work in their campaigns, so don't feel too bad if you fall off the frugal wagon every now and then. Just try to make sure that you have more no-spend days than spending spree days and you will be moving in the right direction.

DEEPER HEALING: BUILD A WAR CHEST

Medieval kings and queens would always have a war chest, which was an accumulation of excess money that had been set aside specifically for the purpose of conducting war campaigns and for the defence of the nation. Should a country happen to be threatened in some way, woe betide the monarch who presented an empty war chest to their people!

The war chest was essential for security. It meant that a nation could afford to defend and protect itself, or ride to the defence of a poorer country, if needs be. Edward 1st, known as Longshanks on account of his 6'2" frame, spent a colossal amount of money waging war against the Scots and building many castles in Wales, in order to subjugate the Welsh people. This simply would not have been possible had he not built up a significant war chest to fund these endeavours.

Your personal war chest is an accumulation of excess money that you can use to see you through troubled times or a challenging situation, if you lost your job for instance, or became ill and couldn't work for a long period of time. It should be viewed as a part of your personal arsenal of self-care, for when you have a well-lined war chest, you can handle most battles that life throws your way, much more easily.

It must be said that some people find it extremely difficult to hang onto excess cash. It trickles through their fingers like sand. There is usually a sound psychological reasoning behind this. Excess money can make you a target and flashing the cash in public is the quickest way to get mugged! With this type of reasoning in mind, it can often seem more sensible to *spend* excess money on items that you value, but that no-one else will, whereas everyone values money. Viewed from this perspective, over-spending, or frivolous spending, becomes a strategic defence mechanism: one designed to get rid of the cash that might make you a target, by buying things that only *you* will value and have a use for.

Just like with spending, saving money is a habit. In general, people are usually either natural savers, or natural spenders, but these are both habits that have been, or which can be, acquired. Having a financial cushion or war chest of excess money means that you can meet unexpected bills and expenses more easily, plus it will increase your sense of financial security in knowing that should an emergency arise, you have the funds available to take care of it.

Saving money should be one of your financial priorities, even if you have debts. Paying money into a savings account each month means that you are creating the habit of acquiring and holding onto your personal wealth. You can start with a small amount of money each month, that you won't really miss. The important thing is that you develop the habit of setting money aside each month and not touching it.

See your savings account as your personal war chest. Over time, you can increase the monthly amounts you save, also put any additional income you earn from overtime etc., into your savings account too. In this way you are building yourself a healthy war chest and ensuring your future financial wellbeing. Longshanks would definitely approve!

CHAPTER 13
CREATIVE THERAPY FOR WELLBEING

The creative arts are often used in the therapy room because they help people to over-ride their inner critic, allowing them to express themselves more freely. This kind of creative self-care is good for when you are feeling stressed, anxious, depressed or worried about something. There are many tools used in creative therapy. The ideas in this chapter are just some of them, and you might prefer to do something else instead, which is fine. If you have a passion for flowers for instance, try using flower arranging as a form of creative therapy. Art, music, writing, dance, sculpture, needlecraft, candle making and so on, can all become a part of your self-care and personal healing journey. Creative therapy is where self-care and healing meets the free play of the inner child, so have fun with it.

DISSOCIATION

When people get very stressed, or they are dealing with the aftermath of trauma, such as the flashbacks associated with PTSD for example, they can often feel like they are no more than a floating head. Everything is going on in their mind, but no-one else can see what is happening to them. They become very disconnected, both from themselves and from the world around them. We call this disconnected feeling, *dissociation* and it can last anywhere from a few minutes, to several months, even years in extreme cases. Reconnecting with the body during such times helps the dissociation to pass more quickly, so anything that brings your awareness back into your body is recommended, from hot baths, long walks and exercise, to creative endeavours. While dissociation is a common symptom of deep trauma and PTSD, it also has its own symptoms and it presents itself in several ways:

- The Floating Head feeling that we just mentioned

- Racing thoughts that just won't stop

- Feeling disconnected from yourself, other people and the world at large

- A blurred sense of your environment, as if everything is swathed in a thick grey fog, without colour

- Fragmented or distorted memories

- Amnesia and losing chunks of time that you just don't remember

- De-personalization, when you just don't feel like you anymore and have no real sense of identity

- De-realization, which is when everything feels like a dream

Living through a period of dissociation can be very difficult. It is overwhelming and disorientating, regardless of how long it lasts. You might even think that you are going mad, but you're not, you're just experiencing the dissociative phenomenon associated with acute stress and deep trauma. The good news is, that reconnecting with your body really does help, pulling your awareness out of your overly triggered mind.

WORK WITH YOUR HANDS

Most types of creativity involve working with the hands in some way. Painting, sketching, knitting, carpentry, baking, needlework, making delicious smelling candles or soaps – all of these activities are done by working with your hands, which draws your attention away from the turmoil in your mind and brings it back into your body. In essence that is the point of creative therapeutic wellbeing. It isn't just a handy-craft or a project, it is a way to switch off the damaging effects of trauma and to over-ride the symptoms of it, such as flashbacks. This type of creative therapy is also very gentle in nature, so it is perfect for those days where you have very little energy, but you just want to do something that can make you feel better quite quickly.

DEEPER HEALING: DRAW YOUR MOOD

One of the most effective forms of creative therapy is sketching out your mood in some way, using art therapy to literally draw out your inner darkness and pin it down on the page. Using a large sketch pad, simply draw how you feel. You might draw a wall, or a cage if you feel blocked or trapped. You might cover the whole page in black charcoal because your mood is so dark and you can't see a spark of light. Whatever you sketch is fine, because this is just where you are right now. It's a beginning.

Repeating this process and drawing out the darkness onto paper each day, helps to filter it out of your mind. It pins the mood and the dark thoughts down on the page, where you can see them and know exactly what you're dealing with. The next step is to draw the same image, but put in some way to deal with it – so you might add a bulldozer to knock down the wall, or Harry Potter to wave his wand and take you through the wall into Diagon Alley! This helps you to see that you are in control of your emotions.

You can use this creative therapy tool to get a handle on depression. Sketch it out day by day, adding different ways to deal with the darkness, effectively lifting your mood as you work. You can be as creative and as humorous as you like – there are no limits to what you draw. Try it and see if it helps. You can also use the same principle to get creatively messy with paint. Use brushes, your hands or even your feet, to lay your emotions down onto a large sheet of paper. Have fun with it.

SIMPLE SELF-CARE: COMFORT SCARF OR BLANKET

There are many different types of needlecraft that you can incorporate into your self-care, but this exercise is for those of you who enjoy knitting or crochet and who have a knowledge of the basics. For this project you are going to make a scarf or a small blanket, the choice is yours.

Wrapping up in something warm and snuggly offers a sense of comfort and safety, because subconsciously, it reminds us of being swaddled as babies, meaning that it has the same effect as a hug. Furthermore, making a comforting item for a loved one means that, not only do you have the pleasure of making the garment itself, but you have the additional joy of knowing that they will think of you whenever they wear it. You can pour your love and protection into every stitch, as you will soon see.

To begin, take a trip to your local yarn shop and browse around. Take in the sights and smells of the environment, notice how it is like stepping into the very heart of a beautiful rainbow. Breathe in the scent of fresh new wool. Next decide what you are going to make, a scarf or a blanket.

For a scarf you will need approximately 250 - 300gms of double-knitting wool in the colour of your choice and a pair of size 6 knitting needles. If you are making the scarf for a loved one, be sure to ask them for their colour preferences first. To crochet a small blanket, you will need around 500gms of yarn and a 5mm crochet hook. You can use wool remnants in a variety of colours, or pick a colour that sparks joy. You are going to be working with this yarn for quite some time, so it should be something that is easy on the eyes. Take your colourful loot home with you and you are ready to begin creating the comforting garment.

You can use any kind of stitch that you are adept at. Use plain knitting, or a simple rib pattern for a scarf, for instance, and make it in your preferred width and length. For the blanket, you can knit or crochet lots of small granny squares and then sew them together to form a blanket. Whatever you choose to make, try not to over complicate it, so avoid intricate patterns and stitches. Keep it simple enough that you can do it without much concentration.

Pick up your needlecraft project whenever you are feeling particularly stressed or dissociated. As you knit, visualize the comfort and warmth that the garment will provide, either to yourself or to a loved one. Often, hand-making something for someone you love, increases the pleasure and the motivation to keep going.

WITCHY WAYS: ENCHANT THE GARMENT
As you craft the garment, repeat the following mantra every now and then, to set your magical intention into the stitches. In this way you are creating an enchanted garment, filled with love and light.

Love and respect in every stitch, this garment keeps me/you safe

Keep it close and wear it well, for protection within is vouchsafed

SIMPLE SELF-CARE: HEALING SOAPS
Making your own soaps means that you can imbue them with the healing and self-care properties of your choice, using flowers and essential oils that align with your intention. This gives an added level of magic to your magical baths and personal care. All you need is 200gms of soap base (you can find plant based vegan varieties that are cruelty free) some kind of mould, and the essential

oils and dried flowers of your choice. Here are some flowers and their self-care benefits for you to choose from.

- Lavender for healing

- Pink roses for self-love

- Red roses for romantic love

- Peppermint for energy

- Rosemary for a calm mind and remembrance

- Daisy or camomile for playfulness and the inner child

- Buttercup for radiance and confidence

- Forget-me-not for memory issues

- Poppies for insomnia

- Pansies for overcoming grief

To make the soap, place a pan of water on a low heat, then put the soap base into a heatproof jug and place the jug in the pan of water. Stir the mixture to help it melt, and add 10-15 drops of your chosen essential oil. As you stir say:

I stir in goodness, I stir in calm

I stir in peace, to this healing balm

Keep stirring until all the lumps are gone and the fragrance has been mixed in thoroughly. Next, carefully pour the soap base into the mould. Arrange the dried flowers in the soap mixture before it cools, then leave the soap overnight to set. Once it is hard, remove it from the mould and use it in your magical baths and shower routine.

SIMPLE SELF-HELP: A SELF-LOVE CANDLE
For this project you will need a sheet of ready to roll beeswax, in a colour that makes you think of self-love, so you could use pink, red or your favourite colour. You will also need a length of candle wick, slightly longer than the sheet of beeswax and either rose, lavender or ylang ylang essential oil.

First anoint the candle wick with a few drops of the essential oil to give it a natural fragrance, then lay the wick along one edge of the sheet of beeswax, making sure that the wick is over-hanging the wax at one end. Now gently begin to roll the wax, tucking the wick into the fold as you do so. Keep rolling the wax as you say: I love and respect myself. As you continue to roll, you will see that a candle takes shape. You can anoint the finished candle with more essential oil if you want to. Stand the candle in a suitable holder, light the wick and say:

I surround myself in love and respect

I burn brighter day by day

I show my strength, I speak my truth

Self-love lights my way.

WRITING THERAPY

Getting your ideas, worries, troubles and traumas down on the page can be a very cathartic experience. Turning bad experiences into works of poetry, prose and song can also help to transform how you feel about them too. It's no accident that some of the most beautiful and successful songs have come from the personal heart break of the song-writers.

Art can transform pain into poetry, sadness into song and the process of writing, serves to process your inner-most feelings. You have already made a start on this with the healing journal that you have been making notes in throughout the course of this book, but now you can delve a little deeper into this incredibly rewarding form of creative therapy.

DON'T BIN IT, FILE IT!

Imagine if you never emptied your kitchen bin, how much rubbish would accumulate over the course of a week or a month. Pretty soon it would be a revolting, disgusting, smelly mess and something that you would want to avoid. Unfortunately, that is exactly how many people treat their bad memories – they leave them in the bin of their mind, to pile up and pollute their life.

If you never empty your mental bin, eventually all that rubbish is going to spill over into your daily life. It could manifest as a mental health condition, physical illness, addiction etc., but one way or another, it will start to make its presence known. Traumatic events and dark emotions need to be filed somewhere. Where better than in your healing journal, where they can do you no harm? Use the following therapeutic writing exercises to help you take out the trash.

SIMPLE SELF-CARE: MAKE A WORRY LIST
Making a list of all your worries can help you to put them into some sort of perspective. It can also help you to group them together and prioritize them, in order of what requires your

attention first and what can wait a little while. Sometimes, seeing your worries written down can also highlight when you are over-reacting or catastrophizing. This is a good exercise to do just before you go to bed, to get all your worries down on paper before you go to sleep.

DEEPER HEALING: FILE YOUR FLASHBACKS

If you suffer from flashbacks, amnesia or fragmented memories, then writing them down will give you back a sense of control. A flashback isn't quite the same as a normal memory - it isn't just a case of sitting there and reminiscing about times past. Flashbacks are like an assault on your mind. You have no control over them at all, you cannot make them stop and there is usually no warning as to when one will show up to ruin your day. They leave you feeling exhausted, shaken, trembling in a cold sweat and totally drained of energy. Living with flashbacks is a horrible experience, not least because they can take you completely unawares and make your life a misery.

However, if you were to write down the flashbacks each time they happen, soon you will have a written record of everything your mind has been holding onto and what it is trying to tell you. Repressed memories can be distressing, but they are better out than in! Believe it or not, flashbacks are actually a sign of recovery, so take heart and pin the little blighters down on the page. In this way you will be able to see the progress you make.

For example, you might start off by having several flashbacks a day, every day, sometimes on a loop. Over time, as you write them all down, you may come to notice that you are going days, weeks, then maybe even months, without having a single flashback. This is progress! It is the healing process at work, as a direct result of the therapeutic writing you have been doing, but you might not spot it unless you get into the habit of documenting your flashbacks each time they appear.

DEEPER HEALING: WRITE A LETTER TO YOUR YOUNGER SELF

Writing a letter to a younger version of yourself is a great way to connect with your inner child. Obviously, if you have childhood trauma, then you need to be a bit careful with this one and make sure that there is someone you trust close by, as you do this exercise.

- Pick an age from your past – try to pick an age that has some significance to you, or a time when you were on the brink of a big change.

- Write a letter to who you were then, as if you are writing to a very dear friend.

- Include advice and words of wisdom that you want to offer to your younger self

- Reassurance that everything turns out okay in the end and that you survived/thrived.

- Acknowledge how you have tried to meet the needs of your younger self. So you might write *I bought that piano that you always wanted. I play every day now.* Or perhaps *I see a therapist every month and I'm telling your story.*

- Thank your younger self for the lessons and skills learned in childhood that you still use today e.g. *I still go horse-riding and I want to thank you for all the effort you put in to learning to ride.*

- Ease the worries of your younger self if you can i.e. *Don't worry about not being able to do algebra. You're never going to need it anyway. I haven't used it since I was your age! It's not worth crying over. You're better at other things. Concentrate on those instead.*

- When you are finished, sign the letter and then read it through. You can either keep it, or burn it and scatter the ashes to the wind.

CHAPTER 14
THE PSYCHOLOGY OF SELF-IMAGE

Self-image is about so much more than outward appearance. It isn't just about the clothes you wear, or the perfume you like to use, though those things can play a small part in how you present yourself to the world. Your self-image encompasses your perceived capabilities, talents, ambitions, strengths, weaknesses and personality traits. It is about how you see yourself, how you think other people see you and also, who you would like to become in the future.

Your self-image is developed at a young age, with the main aspects of it being in place long before you reach adolescence, which is usually when people become more aware of their image and how they fit into the world around them. This is what makes teenagers seem very awkward, as they come to terms with who they are, versus who they would like to be, influenced by what the beauty standards of the media tell them they *should* be.

Personal development is an on-going process. You are never really a finished article, because you are always growing, changing and evolving as you experience life and the changes that it inevitably brings. The things that you enjoyed in your twenties, may not be things that still interest you in your fifties. However, going through life with the attitude of '*why should I change?*' is an indication of a fairly narcissistic attitude. If you know that you have faults, it is your personal responsibility to work on those faults, so that you can become a better version of yourself and less annoying to others!

Self-image then, is the collective result of your life experiences, personal relationships, career choice and external influences such as the media. It actually has very little to do with what is in your wardrobe! This is why buying lots of new clothes only makes you feel happy for a short while, because it doesn't change the inner landscape of your self-image, which is a psychological concept, not a sartorial one.

PARENTAL INJUNCTIONS AND SELF-IMAGE

In the world of psychotherapy, we often talk about parental injunctions, which are subliminal messages passed down to us from parents, teachers and care-givers. These messages are both given and received outside of awareness, which basically means that neither child nor parent knows that it is going on. These messages are taking place on an entirely subconscious level. Again, this isn't about blaming the parents, it is just something that happens. Your parents will have had their own injunctions too, passed down from your grandparents.

What do we mean by an injunction? An injunction is a type of psychological programming which leads the child to behave in a particular way. Usually beginning with the word '*Don't*' injunctions are designed to infringe on a child's freedom, but because they are given at a subconscious level, the child cannot openly rebel against the injunctions, they simply accept the unspoken command and live their life accordingly. Knowing what the injunctions are and how they affect self-image, can help you to identify the injunctions on which you base your behaviour and decisions in adulthood. There are twelve injunctions in all, which are listed below, along with their self-care antidotes. See which ones strike a chord with you. It is not uncommon to have more than one, with different injunctions being passed down from different parents and care-givers.

DON'T EXIST

This is the injunction given by an emotionally distant parent or one who was simply too busy to look after you. They might have dropped you off with various baby-sitters, or arranged for you to stay in after school clubs because they were working. It could also be that you were an unwanted child and your parents made sure that you knew this, maybe even referring to you as a mistake. Perhaps your mother told you dark tales of her labour experience when she gave birth to you, blaming you for her pain. We call this *Torn Mother Syndrome* and it often comes with a *Don't Exist* injunction.

What does all this mean for your self-image? Well, it is likely that you try to remain as invisible and in the background as possible. You are the shrinking violet. You might have feelings of worthlessness, uselessness or suicidal ideation. You always feel as if you are an inconvenience, in the way, that you are too much trouble, or that you don't belong.

SELF-CARE ANTIDOTE:
Own your space! Learn to expand your body-language, using dance or martial arts. Let people know that you are around by wearing brighter colours or being more expressive in your actions. You have every right to exist and to live well whilst existing!

DON'T BE YOU

A *Don't Be You* injunction can come about when a parent has a child of the opposite sex to the one they actually wanted. So if you always had to behave like a tomboy to please your father, or if you had to be a bit of a softy and a mummy's boy, to keep your mother's attention, then you are likely to have this injunction. This could have been compounded if the toys and games they bought for you were ones that their *ideal* child would have had, even if they were toys that didn't really interest you. It could also be that you were constantly being compared to a sibling in an unfavourable way, such as '*Why can't you be more like…*'. Again this gives the injunction *Don't Be You*, don't be who you are, be something else instead.

SELF-CARE ANTIDOTE:
Write down all the things that are unique about you, all the things that you are good at and why these are important. Know that it is okay to be who you are, you don't need to try and be anything else. As an adult, you are in charge of your life and you can be anything you want to be.

DON'T BE A CHILD

This injunction often comes about when you are forced to grow up too soon, either by circumstance or because your parents treated you like a mini adult, confiding in you and putting too much responsibility on young shoulders. It could be that you had to look after younger siblings, or that you were a carer for a sick parent. It could be that a parent confessed all their adult secrets to you, such as affairs or misdemeanours. Often this injunction is given by a narcissistic parent who is very immature, maybe acting like a wayward teenager well into their middle or advanced years, and expecting you to take on the responsibilities that they let slide, or pick up the pieces of the mess they make. In this scenario, there is only space for one child and the parent has decided to claim that role for themselves. This is also a common injunction in the children of parents who suffer with addiction.

If this resonates with you, it is highly likely that you are in the habit of taking on too much responsibility. You might find it difficult to relax and let your hair down. You might have control issues too, where you always need to be in charge and you don't trust anyone else to take the lead. Perfectionism is likely to be something you struggle with. You probably find it very difficult to ask for, or accept, help.

SELF-CARE ANTIDOTE:
Allow yourself to have fun! Let the reins of control slip a little bit and delegate some responsibility to others. Use Free Play to reconnect with your inner child – what would *they* like to do today? What did you always wish you could do as a kid, but were never allowed? Take steps to do that thing and enjoy yourself.

DON'T GROW UP

If you are the youngest child in the family, chances are that you have this injunction to some degree. The *Don't Grow Up* message is given in order to protect the parent, who needs to be needed. Maybe they are afraid of being left all alone, or they are immature and need you to be a *friend*, rather than a child who will grow into adulthood and forge a life of your own. Maybe they fear your burgeoning sexuality and attractiveness, which feels like a threat to them. Whatever their reasons, the message is always the same – *stay young, stay small, stay helpless, stay close, stay with me.*

This injunction may manifest in a myriad of ways. You might dress in an immature way, or your parents may infantilize you well into adulthood. You might never leave home or start relationships of your own. You might behave in a more child-like way when you are with the parent who gave you this injunction, but you are quite mature in other aspects of your life. You might have developed a learned fear of your sexuality and the power of your own sex appeal.

SELF-CARE ANTIDOTE:
Start to work on your independence. Go to places alone, take up a new hobby or start a course of education. Reassess your wardrobe

and see if you are dressing in a way that is age-appropriate. Try to let go of any childish habits you have been holding onto. Take steps to increase your levels of elegance and sophistication.

DON'T SUCCEED

This is often the injunction that a failed parent will give to their child. It's a way of saying *'Don't do better than me, don't make more money than me, don't show me up by becoming a success when I am a failure'*. It can even come from parents who have achieved a certain amount of success through extremely hard work and who now resent how much easier life is for their children as a result! If your parents struggled for money, yet you are making a comfortable living there might be some resentment of your improved fortune, which comes through in this injunction. Conversely, if you lose a job you love, your parents may offer support with so much glee that you wonder if they are glad you've been knocked down. Schadenfreude is usually at work here. The *Don't Succeed* injunction is the crabs in a bucket scenario in play, where if one crab climbs up to escape the bucket, the other crabs drag it back down again, to keep it trapped in the bucket with them.

If you have this injunction, then you are at a very high risk of constantly self-sabotaging. You might have all the best intentions, but somehow you always miss the boat, miss the deadline, mess up the interview, fail the exam etc. You might waste or ignore opportunities that come your way.

SELF-CARE ANTIDOTE:
What would you do if you were guaranteed success? Imagine that you have achieved a big goal and you are about to break that news to your parents. How does this make you feel? Nervous, worried, scared of rejection? Now imagine that they are delighted by the news! How does that make you feel? You have every right to

succeed in your own life, so set a small goal and begin to plan and take the steps necessary to achieve it.

JUST DON'T DO IT

Probably the most all-encompassing injunction of them all, this one refers to the fact that you shouldn't do anything! It comes from a place of inflated fear on the part of an over-protective parent, the kind who didn't want to take you to the park when you were small in case you fell off the climbing frame and hurt yourself! If you were never allowed to go sledging, dancing or out on your own then you probably have this injunction. If everything was presented to you as a great risk, or if your parent always stepped in as you attempted something difficult and did it for you, then a *Just Don't* injunction is in play. It implies that you shouldn't try to do anything at all, because you might get hurt or upset or disappointed.

In terms of self-image this one is really damaging, because it leads to a sense of incompetence, uselessness and a life that seems frozen in one place. You might feel that you can't do anything right, so why bother trying? This injunction leaves you stuck and stagnating, too afraid to make a move in any direction in case you get it wrong and something bad happens. Mistakes are part of life and you need to allow yourself to make a few. And here's the truth your parent *didn't* want you to know – making little mistakes can also be a lot of fun!

SELF-CARE ANTIDOTE:
Life is meant to be fluid, not stagnant. Instead of worrying that you might do the wrong thing, give yourself *permission* to do the wrong thing, to make mistakes, to not get things right first time. Mistakes are how you learn and how you move forward. Instead of telling yourself *Just Don't*, tell yourself *Yes I Can!* Give yourself

a small challenge to accomplish this week. Gradually build up to bigger challenges and watch your sense of competence grow. In this instance, if you *can* do it, then you *should* do it, because it's good for you to try new things.

DON'T BE IMPORTANT

This type of injunction is usually given by parents who have never felt important in their own lives. It can often go hand in hand with the *Don't Succeed* injunction, leading to a double whammy of belittling. It can also come from care-givers who either distrust authority, or who fawn in the face of it. They are not comfortable with any kind of authority, so they naturally don't want their child to grow up to become an authority figure, because then they wouldn't be able to relate to you. Furthermore, this injunction is designed to keep you small, inferior and down-trodden.

If you have this injunction you might find yourself living a very small, safe life. You might have had issues with authority figures yourself, or find that you become nervous when in their presence. You might avoid any type of responsibility, especially in the workplace, or find it difficult to ask for what you want or need. Speaking up is likely to be difficult for you, leading to acute shyness, possibly even panic attacks when you are expected to do any kind of public speaking.

SELF-CARE ANTIDOTE:
It's time for you to step out of the shadows and show yourself more. Learn to speak up. It's okay to ask for what you want. It's okay to take steps to get your needs met. Experiment with pushing the boundaries of your comfort zone – could you volunteer for a little extra responsibility at work, or help out at a charity? Could you speak up more, ordering food in a restaurant instead of letting your partner do it? Find your feet, find your voice and know that

you have an important role to play in your own life and in the lives of your loved ones too.

DON'T BELONG

A *Don't Belong* injunction often comes from parents who view their child as somehow different from other children and not usually in a flattering way! It is a classic case of 'othering' and it leads to the child feeling like they have no place, either within the family, or in wider groups in society. It can frequently be a factor in mixed race families, where the children might grow up to feel that they cannot relate to either side of their family and that they don't belong anywhere.

If you have this injunction, then your self-image is likely to be one of isolation, never fitting in anywhere. You may feel ostracised or out of the loop, never one to be accepted by the inner circle, the clique or the cool kids. You might describe yourself as a loner or a lone wolf. Others might see you as being unsociable or anti-social. You are forever on the outside, looking in, watching everyone else gather together, while you remain out in the cold. It is also possible that you suffer with some degree of social anxiety.

SELF-CARE ANTIDOTE:
Find your tribe! It may be that the reason you feel you don't belong is because you have yet to find your tribe, so get out and start looking for people you have a shared interest with. Join a club, go to a class or a gym. Smile at people when you get there, so that you look approachable. Admit that you are nervous and someone is likely to take you under their wing. Do nice things for other people and have patience with yourself as you learn to become more socially adept.

DON'T BE CLOSE

This injunction comes from parents who are not comfortable with any kind of affection, either physical or emotional. They don't like hugs and kisses: they don't say *I love you*. They remain detached and distant, regardless of the circumstances. They can come across as being very cold, aloof and uncaring. Different generations have different expectations of what is acceptable in terms of showing affection and a *Don't Be Close* injunction tends to come from someone who is not very demonstrative of their feelings and expects the same from other people.

If you have this injunction, then you might have a deep fear of rejection. You might have reached out to your parents on many occasions, but never received the affection you craved as a child. In adulthood, this transcribes in one of two ways. Either you emulate your parent and become equally uncomfortable with signs of affection, or you over-compensate and become someone who smothers with love, to the point where that intensity could drive people away. You might find it difficult to express your feelings or tell people you love them. Trust is also likely to be a big issue for you, as you can't trust anyone to be there for you in the way that you need. You feel that you are unlovable.

SELF-CARE ANTIDOTE:
Open up. Be brave and tell your nearest and dearest how you feel about them. If you tend to smother people, learn to back off a little and give them more space. Show how you feel with acts of service, if you are not comfortable in saying it out loud. Know that you are lovable and that you deserve to love and be loved in return.

DON'T BE WELL/SANE

If your parents lavished attention on you when you were ill, but didn't have a lot of time for you when you were healthy, then you could easily have picked up this injunction. It is a way of getting attention and it can last well into adulthood. It can last a lifetime, for this is where hypochondria begins.

The problem is that as a self-fulfilling prophecy you can actually train your body and mind to develop illness! This in turns leads to a self-image of frailty, delicacy and weakness. You might develop depression or melancholia, existing on a cocktail of medication and participating in a revolving door process of various therapies and treatments. You might fake dizziness or fainting spells to get attention, or to manipulate others. You might feel constantly confused, like everything is far too complicated for you to understand. Life feels like it's all too much, and you're just too frail to handle it. This is nonsense! It is just your injunction talking and you need to over-ride it asap!

SELF-CARE ANTIDOTE:
Develop your strengths – physical, mental and emotional. Go back and re-read the chapter on robustness, because that is what you need to work on. Start to take pride in your resilience, see yourself as having great fortitude, not frailty. Everyone has the odd day when they feel a bit delicate, but don't allow this to become your day to day lifestyle. You are not a character in a Victorian novel, fainting away every five minutes! You are a strong, formidable individual. Own it!

DON'T THINK

A *Don't Think* injunction comes from a parent who constantly belittles or interrupts a child's thought processes. Often the parent is highly educated and intelligent, and they forget that they are interacting with a child whose critical thinking isn't yet fully developed, so they become impatient, leading to the belittling behaviour or to the parent completing the thought process on the child's behalf and providing all the answers.

If you have this injunction, then your self-image might be one of mental inferiority. You feel that you are not as clever as everyone else, or that you will look like a fool if you try to solve a problem and come up with the wrong answer, so you simply stop trying to solve problems! Brain-freeze is common with this injunction. In the long term this leads to under-confidence in all areas, so it really does need to be nipped in the bud.

SELF-CARE ANTIDOTE:
Educate yourself. Find a topic that you love and begin to self-educate on that subject. This will help to over-ride those internal messages that you are not clever, or that you are stupid. You're not. You simply need to train your brain to gather and sift through information, so that you become better at critical analysis and problem solving.

DON'T FEEL

This injunction tends to come from parents with very little emotional intelligence. They might bottle up their feelings, or show their emotions in an inappropriate or disproportionate manner. All this adds up to the Don't Feel injunction, meaning that the child in question also grows up with a lack of emotional intelligence.

If you have this injunction, then it is likely to manifest as anxiety and overwhelm, leading to a self-image of one who is highly-strung, possibly histrionic. You might avoid highly emotive situations such as sick rooms or funerals because you can't handle the emotions they bring up. It is also likely that you become confused about the correct emotional response, meaning that you demonstrate anger, when really you feel upset and should show sadness or sorrow. You might use your image as a form of armour, or to keep people at a distance.

SELF-CARE ANTIDOTE:
Track your emotions. Find out how you respond emotionally to different situations. Are you exhibiting the correct emotion for the situation? Are your emotions in proportion to the event, or do you over- or under- react? Read Chapter 17 on Emotional Intelligence.

As you can see, your self-image has very little to do with the things you choose to wear or how you style your hair. Those are merely the trappings of the psychological self-image you formed during childhood, which is based on your personal injunctions. Understanding how these injunctions can combine to determine how you see yourself and your place in the world, is half the battle to improving your self-image, because now you have the tools you need to over-ride these injunctions and make better decisions for yourself going forward, thus creating a new self-image of your own making.

CHAPTER 15
CREATING A LIFE THAT YOU LOVE

When you are living a life that you love, low mood and depression become less of an issue. When you feel secure in your abilities and content in your lifestyle, there is less to be anxious about. Most people make plans for their holidays or for festive events such as Christmas, yet very few actually sit down and plan out the kind of life they want to lead. Instead, they leave it all up to fate to decide, or they follow the crowd and just go with the flow. If this has led you to a fulfilled and happy life, then there is no problem, but if it hasn't then something obviously needs to change.

DON'T GO WITH THE FLOW

Being relaxed and laid back about life is one thing, but having no sense of direction or self-agency is quite another. You wouldn't get into a boat and just allow the water to take you wherever it wanted to. You would learn how to sail. You would learn how to navigate, decide on a destination and steer the boat in that direction until you reached it. The same should be true for your life.

Drifters tend to be compulsive complainers too, moaning that they never get a break or a leg up and yet they take no steps to facilitate this kind of break-through. They are existing from a Victim standpoint. Even worse, their nearest and dearest often buy into this narrative, supporting their belief that they are hard done by and that successful people have just been very, very lucky. The problem here is that drifting aimlessly wastes a lot of time. It can lead you into jobs you don't like, parenthood before you're ready and marriage or relationships that just happened. It is a very apathetic way to live and it will get you nowhere.

On the other hand, autonomy is like a super power. It gives you a great drive to set goals and press ahead until you achieve them. This might mean going against the grain and it is likely to be uncomfortable at times, but it works. It moves your life forward and keeps your level of achievement fairly consistent.

DESIGN A LIFE YOU LOVE

Have you ever sat down and actually *designed* your life? Have you ever made a five-year plan on paper, or mapped out where you want to be by a certain age? If not, then it's time to make a start! While it's true that you cannot plan for every eventuality, if you have no plan at all in place, then you will be buffeted by the whims of fate, so it is far better to take as much control of your life as is humanly possible and that means creating the kind of lifestyle that suits you best.

Creating a life map can be such a fun exercise. Here you get to dream on the page about all the things you would love to do. While you can create a life plan at any time, I believe that it is essential to make one in the months following a big upheaval of some sort or an unwelcome life change such as bereavement or divorce. Taking charge of your future in this way can become part of the healing process and it helps to at least imagine your way forward. It is also important not to plan too far ahead, as that can be very overwhelming. Stick to five year plans that you remake every four years. Don't wait until you have achieved everything on your current plan before you make a new one, simply move unachieved goals across to the new five-year life map and take it from there.

SIMPLE SELF-CARE: LIFE MAPPING

To begin with, make a list of all the things you want to experience, do and achieve. Be sure to include all aspects of your life, from career, to relationships to leisure and travel. Next split these goals into three sections, as below:

- ***Immediate Goals****: things you can achieve and do in the next 6 months*

- ***Intermediate Goals****: things you plan to achieve in the next 12-24 months*

- ***Long Range Goals****: things you want to complete and do in the next 5 years*

For each section, try to include goals for career, relationships, family, travel, experiences and hobbies. Make sure each section also includes something to achieve, something to do regularly, something to look forward to, a place to visit and something to aim high for. In this way you will remain productive, high achieving and you will keep up the momentum of your life, enjoying new experiences, rather than falling back into a rut. Be aware that these plans need not be elaborate or expensive. For example, you can choose to go for a walk in the woods or local park every week as your regular goal, or plan to get a new pet as an intermediate goal.

WITCHY WAYS: A SPELL FOR A LUCKY BREAK

Moon Phase: perform during the new – full moon

Items required: a gold candle and holder, ylang ylang essential oil

Sometimes all you need is the right person to come along and see your potential, offering you a lucky break and assisting in your transformation and healing journey. To draw this kind of lucky break towards you, anoint a gold candle with ylang ylang oil to attract positive opportunities, light it and repeat the following chant nine times, out loud or in your head, before letting the candle burn down naturally,

A lucky break I seek to find

It comes to me through space and time

I call this opportunity

I'll know it when it comes to me.

FACING THE VOID

Whenever a negative life event happens, often it is followed by some sort of void. This is true regardless of the event. It could be a lost job, the death of a beloved pet, the end of a relationship, the loss of good health. The void is always waiting, just beyond the initial loss and it can be a very scary thing to face up to.

This period of time, when you are staring into the abyss of what used to be and may never be again, can be terrifying. It is usually during this phase that some people begin to self-medicate with drugs and alcohol, because they are looking for a way to escape the void, to ignore it and to find a sense of support in all the wrong places. However, substance abuse and addiction only delays the inevitable and at some stage they will have to face that initial void and the emptiness that was left behind following the loss.

Facing the void is never easy, yet it inevitably follows on from a loss. This is true of any loss, whether it be the loss of a job, a divorce or break-up, or a bereavement. The void triggers your fears for the future, your anxieties and insecurities. It makes you question your identity, for who are you if you don't have that job, that marriage, that family member? The void is like a dark mirror, reflecting your own mortality back at you and forcing you to find an answer to the question: *What now?*

Take heart though, because life is a cycle of birth, death and rebirth. Therefore, if your life has been touched by a death or a loss of some kind, it is only a matter of time before the rebirth takes place. Waiting for life to labour a new beginning is a painful and frustrating process. It might seem as if a new start is way out of reach, but the universe hates an empty void, so something has to come along to fill the space the loss left behind.

Part of facing the void involves letting go. You have to let go of what you have lost before you can move on, though this is easier said than done. But there is also another kind of letting go - that of surrender. You need to be ready to let go and surrender, to just wait and see what life has in store for you next. Believe that you will be blessed with the right kind of opportunities when you are ready to receive them. In the meantime, work the ritual below to help you surrender more easily.

WITCHY WAYS: RITUAL OF SURRENDER
Take a piece of paper and write a list of all the things that you associate with the loss that you want to surrender to the universe. This list could include things like insomnia, depression, sadness, flashbacks, financial worries and so on. What does the abyss look like to you? How is it impacting your life? Take as much time over this as you need and when your list is complete, burn it in a heatproof dish and say:

I hereby surrender all my woeful ways

I move towards brighter days

I surrender my sorrows into the abyss

Let the void transform them into a new bliss.

TIMING IS EVERYTHING

How you manage your time plays a key role in how balanced your life and mental health are. If you take on too much at once, then you will feel like you're spinning plates! It can leave you feeling overwhelmed and exhausted. It can also have a negative impact on your relationships too, as you are never free to spend quality time with your loved ones. If you find yourself talking about how to *juggle* things, and you're *not* a member of a circus, then this is a sign that you are taking on too much! Dial it back a bit. Delegate tasks or just say no.

On the other hand, it is possible to have *too* much time on your hands. If every day feels like a vast wasteland that you have to get through, then you need to address this. Often, it comes about following a very low period, say after a bout of deep depression or a bereavement. It means that the habit of doing nothing has taken hold and while this was useful to begin with, as you cleared the decks so that you could process your feelings on whatever you were going through at the time, as a long term habit it can be very damaging, leading to feelings of worthlessness, isolation and possibly even suicidal thoughts. Feeling lost and aimless is natural after a big upheaval of some kind, but it isn't meant to become how you normally operate.

SIMPLE SELF-CARE: TIME STRUCTURING

We mentioned time structuring briefly at little earlier in the book. Simply put it is the concept of blocking out chunks of time to be set aside for specific events and activities. Using a monthly spread in a diary or calendar is the best way to do this, as you can see quite clearly how much time you have available and how you plan to fill it.

Time structuring doesn't mean filling up every hour of the day. It is a way of making your obligations and responsibilities more manageable, at the same time as factoring in fun things to do so that you have something to look forward to each week, even if that's just meeting a friend for coffee and cake. Factor in self-care pamper days, or relaxing evenings at home curled up with a new book to read. These dates with yourself are just as important as your work schedule or health appointments, so don't neglect to add a few in each month.

Grab your diary or calendar and begin to take charge of actively structuring your time. Make that appointment with the doctor or dentist and write it in. Block out the days that you are working and make those your relaxation evenings. Factor in something fun to do each week, such as seeing a concert, taking a trip to the seaside, a visit to the library or museum, a night out, taking a new class of some sort or having a TV marathon with a box set. Don't take on more than one or two extra responsibilities and events each week. Keep it simple. Keep it steady. Write it all down in your diary and take a firm hold of your life by planning it out, day by day. In this way you avoid both pitfalls of taking on too much and not having enough to do.

DO YOU HAVE RESISTANCE BIAS?

In psychology, we often talk of cognitive biases. Resistance bias is one of the main sticking points when it comes to healing old wounds and making positive change. People who have experienced trauma tend to develop resistance bias as a coping strategy. In a nutshell, resistance bias refers to a habitual tendency towards rejection. It is a deep resistance to any kind of change, even the positive, helpful kind. Signs that you have a degree of resistance bias include:

- Saying no to things out of habit and without due consideration

- Pushing people away when they try to help you

- Refusing invitations with no real reason for doing so

- Not considering that someone might have your best interests at heart

- Severe discomfort around notions of any kind of change

- Unwillingness to step out of your comfort zone, even when that comfort zone is damaging and potentially dangerous

At its heart, resistance bias is a form of self-preservation, which is a powerful component of your survival instinct. It means that people sometimes choose to stay in a miserable rut, because saying no and refusing help has become a habit they can't break.

Resistance bias means that you don't allow yourself time to assess the situation and weigh up the pros and cons *before* you respond – you just say *No* automatically, often before you're even fully aware of what you're rejecting. We see this a lot in romantic situations, when a heartbroken individual refuses to go out on dates, saying no to all invitations and generally resisting any opportunity for romance, for fear that it might make them vulnerable. They become very resistant to giving new love a chance, and even though they might *say* they want to start again, their psychological bias gets in the way, acting as a form of self-sabotage.

Resistance bias stems from a lack of trust in others. It is a lingering aspect of traumatic stress, which makes perfect sense, because saying No to everything, all the time, will certainly keep you safe! However, it will also prevent you from living the life you truly want, so you need to nip it in the bud.

DEEPER HEALING: OVER-RIDE RESISTANCE BIAS

The mind is a powerful thing. It can play tricks on you if you let it. The moment you try to step outside of your comfort zone the brain gets scared and prepares itself to do battle. It throws up impostor syndrome, perceived threat detection and resistance bias, making you hot-foot it back to your comfort zone as fast as possible. It amplifies your negative self-talk so that you might start to believe that negativity to be true, but it isn't true. You deserve to be the best that you can be in all things, in all aspects of your life.

The fastest way to over-ride a resistance bias is to just say yes. Sounds simple, but it isn't, particularly if you have had this bias for a long period of time. Start with small things. Say yes to a cup of coffee with a trusted friend, or yes to an invitation of some kind, because it's time to get a grip on your *No*-ing ways! It's time to actively seek to expand the parameters of your life, to make it bigger, bolder and brighter than ever. It's time to break the knee-jerk reaction of saying *no*, so that you can start saying *Yes* again. *Yes!* to new work opportunities, *yes* to new experiences, *yes* to new places, people and pleasures, *yes* to bold, new adventures. Just say *YES!!!*

CHAPTER 16

SOCIAL MEDIA – A BLESSING AND A CURSE

We live in a world of instant gratification, where practically anything your heart desires can be delivered directly to your door, where people strike up friendships and relationships online, sharing intimate details about their lives with people they have never met in person. All of this convenience has led to a society which lacks patience and may struggle to form real, genuine connections.

The internet can be a wonderful thing, but there is no doubt that it can also have a negative impact on your mental health if you allow it to. Social media is a window into the world of other people. Very little is off limits, as people post about the food they eat, the places they go, the clothes they wear, the trips they take and so on.

This can be extremely inspiring. It's exciting to be able to see exactly what your favourite celebrity is up to on any given day, to see what they are wearing, what projects they are working on, what charities they support etc. The veil of secrecy between the world of the rich and famous and ordinary people has been swept aside, allowing us to see things that once would have been considered trade secrets.

Furthermore, the internet has also made it possible for ordinary people to document their lives too, or even to become social media celebrities in their own right. Gone are the days when you needed a contract with an agency to become a model or a singer. Now all you need is a platform, such as Instagram, TikTok or You Tube and you can begin to attract followers, which in time may help you to generate an income. Many young people now aspire to become a professional You Tuber or internet sensation and they hold this dream as their main career objective. This fairly new industry can be extremely lucrative for those who manage to achieve a high degree of success and it is one area where no qualifications are necessary to succeed. In this sense, the internet has been a great leveller, with social media playing a key role in this type of levelling up.

However, the internet does have a dark side and you cannot put the genie back in the bottle once it is out! Being subjected to a constant barrage of images and information can take its toll on your mental health and self-esteem. As we live more of our lives through some kind of screen, conditions such as social anxiety and dissociation are becoming more prevalent. Advertising is rife on most sites and platforms, and it can be difficult to draw the line between when you are acting on impulse because you have been influenced, or when you are acting from self-agency. So how do you navigate what is, in effect, a mental health minefield? The answer is, with caution and careful consideration.

THE POWER OF INFLUENCE

Influence is the ability to change someone's way of thinking, their habits and desires. In essence it is a form of manipulation, though it is usually so covert, you might not notice it at first. We are all subject to being influenced and this isn't a notion that was invented by social media gurus. It certainly isn't a new concept and people have always been influenced by the various stars and celebrities of the time. Think of Anne Boleyn influencing the fashion for French hoods in the English Court, Princess Diana inspiring droves of young women to take on the Sloane Ranger look, or Queen Victoria popularizing white wedding gowns and black mourning attire, both of which are influences we still adhere to at weddings and funerals today.

The problem occurs, not when you are being influenced by social media, but when you are being influenced in the wrong way, or when that influence is less aspirational and more of a psychological trigger. If watching your favourite social media content makes you feel positive and ready to reach for your own dreams and goals, then that is a positive influence, but if it makes you feel sad, unworthy or lacking in some way, then that is a negative influence. Likewise, if a particular Influencer triggers destructive patterns such as compulsive shopping, under- or over-eating, risky behaviours and so on, then that would indicate that you have been spending time in the presence of a bad influence. Do some self-parenting and separate yourself from this kind of bad influence by unfollowing or muting the account, then cast the following spell to give yourself some magical back up as you wean yourself off such damaging content.

WITCHY WAYS: DIMINISHING SPELL FOR A BAD INFLUENCE

> *Items required: a notepad and pen, cauldron or heat proof bowl, a lighter*
>
> *Timing: perform on a waning moon*

If there is something or someone that you know has a bad influence on you, cast this spell to diminish their power. On a piece of paper, write down the nature of the influence as a complete sentence, so for example: *Social Media Influence on body image*. Next write out the sentence again, leaving out last letter. Repeat this until you are down to a single letter:

> *Social Media Influence on body image*
>
> *Social Media Influence on body imag*

Social Media Influence on body ima

Social Media Influence on body im...

Once you have diminished the sentence, fold the paper into three and light the end with the lighter, then drop it in the cauldron to burn. When the ashes have cooled, scatter them to the winds. Monitor the amount of time you spend around any influences that make you feel bad about yourself.

DOOMSCROLLING

Doomscrolling happens when you have been sucked into the web of news feeds that appear on social media. You might never watch the news on the TV, but you cannot avoid it altogether if you use any kind of social media platform. Constantly checking your phone for updates on negative events can lead to low mood and catastrophizing. The same is true if you are checking your feed to see what people are commenting or saying about you, especially if you know that you are being targeted by bullies and internet trolls.

It begs the question, if you know that the news isn't good, then why keep scrolling and looking for it? In general, doom scrolling occurs when you are looking for answers, when you are feeling scared and nervous and you need confirmation that things aren't as bad as you think. Unfortunately, the news feed tends to reflect the opposite, meaning that you continue searching for some kind of reassurance. In the process, you consume a lot of negative content, which can really bring you down, sometimes even leading to melancholia or mild depression. The more time you spend habitually doom scrolling, the more down in the dumps you become. So how do you get out of a doom scrolling spiral? One idea is to limit the amount of time you spend on your phone, so that you are not falling down the rabbit hole of doom for too long.

This will mitigate the impact somewhat. You could also try to flip your internal switch into seeking out something more positive or unexpected.

SIMPLE SELF-CARE: JOY SCROLLING
If doom scrolling is bad for your mental health, then joy scrolling can give you the lift you need to get out of a dark internet rut. Your brain is designed to notice whatever you are most focused on, so you just need to give it a fresh command. Next time you notice yourself doom scrolling, interrupt the pattern by giving a verbal command to your brain. So you might say something like *I'm looking for funny comments* or *I want to see cute animals*. Try to only click on links to these more positive stories, so that over time, you adapt your algorithms into suggesting happiness-inducing content instead.

THE BENEFITS OF SOCIAL MEDIA AND THE INTERNET

While the internet can be a dark place at times, it can also be very beneficial. Never has it been easier to keep in contact with friends and family, no matter where in the world they might live. Technology means that we can maintain strong connections with loved ones who are working away or who are on holiday in another country. Distance isn't the great barrier to relationships that it once was and long distance romances now stand a better chance of success, thanks to the internet and social media. This kind of connectivity means that we can create whole communities entirely online, made up of people who might never have come together otherwise. It's also a useful tool for people who are housebound, for whatever reason, allowing them to maintain a sense of sociability as they interact online with friends, family and service providers, such as counsellors and therapists. This kind of remote access to services is becoming increasing popular and a whole slew of online-only therapy practices are springing up, at a time when renting premises becomes increasingly expensive.

There is also a political aspect too, as social media platforms are used to mobilize members of the public in peaceful demonstrations and petitions. This kind of *power to the people* means that social media plays a key role in activism and in turn, social reform. Due to its far-reaching potential, social media is one of the best ways to raise awareness of an issue, as people share posts, and important information is distributed quickly and effectively. This can be especially useful for charities and other organisations that work to support a noble cause of some kind. But perhaps the main benefit to the individual is that of education.

SELF-EDUCATION AND ACADEMIA

The invention of the internet means that it has never been easier for people to educate themselves. In the past, there was the educated ruling class and the uneducated, more ignorant lower class. If you were born into a low income family and the expense of university was beyond your budget, or that of your parents, then you would go through life with only the basic education you had in school, and maybe not even that. Ignorance was forced upon you by circumstance. It was an accident of birth. These days however, ignorance is more of a personal choice, as most people now have access to the internet and so self-education is always an option. This effectively means that you can study any topic that interests you, in your own home and in your own time. There are no curriculums to adhere to, and you study entirely at your own pace. There are also no set texts to read, so you will never have to read anything that bores you!

Of course, self-educating will never have the status that a degree brings with it, and a formal university education commands respect in a way that self-education does not, so it has that as an advantage. However, self-education does demonstrate a willingness, and the discipline, to learn. It indicates a proactive attitude, a degree of mental agility and a commitment to personal development, plus it can be a lot of fun too. Studying a topic that you are passionate about is one of the joys of life. Academia is for everyone, though not necessarily in an academic setting, which doesn't suit everybody, yet everyone has the right to educate themselves on the things that interest them. The internet helps to make that possible.

DEEPER HEALING: SELF-EDUCATE

People often have a very negative association with any kind of education, particularly if they didn't like school, but self-education is a wonderful habit to adopt. It is just one aspect of a commitment to life-long learning, which is the intellectual right of every human being. You are entitled to learn and grow, to become a better, more informed version of yourself. Enlightenment begins with the application of reason, the development of individualism and a healthy amount of scepticism which prevents gullibility. Make a commitment to begin self-educating today. Think of a subject that interest you. It need not be a traditional academic subject, just something you have a passion for, be it art, music, sport, dance, history, witchcraft or popular psychology. Pick a topic and begin to learn more about it. Read books about it, watch documentaries, visit exhibits and so on. Make notes as you learn, so that you retain the information. View it as your personal project and begin to see yourself as someone who enjoys academia in your own way.

WITCHY WAYS: ACADEMIA STUDY SPELL

Studying isn't always easy. It takes discipline, consistency and the ability to self-motivate. It can also take a little time for you to ease yourself into a new study session, as you are asking your mind to move away from the mundane cares of the world, into a higher, more scholastic frame of mind. Use this simple spell to assist you in this scholarly transcendence. As you light your study candles say the following incantation:

I kindle the light of knowledge this hour

To impart upon me a Wiccan's power

I use this power in love and light

As I study and learn, new knowledge burns bright.

COMPARISON KILLS JOY

The internet and social media can help to foster the habit of comparison. Comparing your life, body, looks or economic status with the things you see online is the quickest way to destroy your self-esteem. Bear in mind that social media is a highlight reel, where people show the best parts of their lives. No-one's life is perfect, no matter what it might look like on social media. Everyone is struggling with something, so try not to let unfavourable comparisons diminish your light. It is highly likely that there is someone in the world who wishes they could have the life you already enjoy.

CHAPTER 17
EMOTIONAL INTELLIGENCE

E motional intelligence is the ability to control your emotional response to the situations in which you find yourself. Too often people tend to give knee-jerk reactions to things, rather than offering a more considered response. This can lead to an escalation of conflict as tempers inevitably flare. Other people might tear up and cry at the slightest provocation, or become indignantly offended where no offense was intended.

Understanding your own emotions, means that in turn you will be better equipped to understand and empathise with the emotions of others. Identifying your feelings will enable you to ensure that your emotional response is appropriate and proportionate to the situation, while developing a sense of inner poise means fewer melt-downs.

HISTRIONIC BEHAVIOUR

We all know people who simply cannot keep their emotions in check and who go through life in a constant state of emotional turmoil which they broadcast to the world. This is not simply a case of someone who is upset, or who has a short fuse, rather it is a compulsive need for attention, which they achieve by behaving in a dramatic and hysterical way. There are tears, tantrums, emotional blackmail and threats of violence or self-harm, which are all utilised to get everyone's attention. Histrionic types usually play to an audience, but not always. They are easily offended and easily triggered, existing in a semi-permanent state of indignation. Saying that they are huffy, would be to put it mildly! This kind of behaviour comes from someone with little to no emotional intelligence. They have no concept of the fact that there is a time and a place for private discussions, so they play it all out in public, as if they are actors in a soap opera. In the short term they get the attention that they crave, which is why they keep doing it, but in the long term, they are likely to be ruled by their emotions indefinitely unless they take steps to improve their emotional intelligence.

If you can relate to this type of behaviour, then you need to address your emotional incontinence because living from a histrionic standpoint is extremely draining and damaging to your relationships and career prospects. The tips and exercises in this chapter will help you to become more aware of the emotions you are feeling, so that you can express them in a much healthier way.

WHY EMOTIONAL INTELLIGENCE IS IMPORTANT

As social creatures, humans depend on being able to interact with others in a harmonious way. This becomes much easier when you can manage your own emotions, when you can recognise them bubbling up under the surface. It also means that you can recognise those same emotions bubbling up in other people. Recognising the signs that someone is about to lose their temper means that you can take steps to calm the situation. Think back to when you were a child. What were the signs that your parents were losing patience with you and you were about to get a ticking off? Did you heed these warning signs by moderating your behaviour? If so, this is an indication of emotional intelligence at work.

Managing your emotions and the emotions of others is a key life-skill to have. It means that you will recognise when someone is trying to push your buttons and rile you up. There are many people out there who get a kick out of pushing other people's buttons. They thrive on the reaction they provoke. With emotional intelligence you can more easily recognise these people and take steps to be unshakable in their presence. Emotional intelligence means that such people just don't get to you anymore, so it reduces the amount of drama you have to contend with.

This is important in group dynamics, such as in the workplace or in family situations, where there are lots of people, all having to come to together and interact from different emotional states. Being able to recognise when someone is feeling low means that you can help to take the pressure off them a little bit, and vice versa. In this way, harmony is restored and productivity is maintained.

SIMPLE SELF-CARE: ASSESS YOUR EMOTIONS
Regularly check in with yourself by answering the following questions in your journal:

- *What am I feeling right now?*

- *What is the name for this feeling, what emotion is it?*

- *How is it affecting my behaviour?*

- *Is this emotion appropriate to the situation?*

- *Is my emotional response proportionate to the situation, or am I over-reacting?*

- *Have I been triggered by an external event? (E.g. a bad day, a disagreement, a meeting at work etc.)*

- *Have I been triggered by an internal event? (E.g. flashbacks, bad dreams, low mood, hormones, anniversary effect etc.)*

- *Am I being provoked by someone? Is this provocation deliberate?*

- *Is there someone who is feeding off my emotions? Who?*

- *Is there someone who nurtures a sense of calm in me? Who?*

- *How can I release this emotion in a positive way?*

- *What can I do to make myself feel better in this moment?*

Assessing your emotions in this way means that you will have a clear idea of where the emotion is coming from, meaning that you can then identify ways of tackling it in the future. For instance, if someone is deliberately trying to provoke you, then you can take steps to avoid them or you can confront them and tell them to stop. You can also cast the spell below.

WITCHY WAYS: SPELL TO CUT AWAY A BUTTON-PUSHER!

Items required: black thread or string, cauldron or heat proof bowl, scissors, matches

Timing: perform this spell as the moon wanes

Whenever you form a relationship, be it personal or professional, you create a psychic connection with that person. This is as true for someone that you don't like as it for the relationships you have with loved ones. Our emotions, good and bad, create enmeshments with other people. In magic we refer to these links as psychic cords. In order to be free of someone's influence over you, you will need to cut the cords, whether that person is an ex-partner or you need to cut ties with an old workplace so that you can move forward in your life, the cords need to be cut so that your life can progress in a positive way. Cord cutting is one of the oldest forms of uncrossing spell. To begin with, sit and think about the person who is provoking you. Anyone who makes you feel strong emotions such as love, hate, envy etc. has an influence over you, so if they are no longer part of your life, you need to cut away that influence. Anyone who keeps trying to provoke you should hold no place in your life or your mind, so cut them out. Now think of all the ways in which you were connected to them – mentally, emotionally, sexually, physically – and use the thread to wrap around yourself the areas that represent this connection, so wrap the cords around your chest for love, round your hips for a sexual connection and so on. Tie each set of cords in place. This ritual can feel very uncomfortable as you realise how ensnared you are to the other person. When you feel ready, pick up the scissors and begin to cut away all of the cords as you say:

I sever the ties that bound us together

I free myself as these bonds I now sever

When you have cut away all the cords, drop them in the cauldron and light them with a match. As you watch the cords burn, know that they are freeing you from someone who is trying to provoke you in some way, leaving you free to move on with your day.

YOUR EMOTIONS AFFECT OTHER PEOPLE

Your moods can have a deep impact on the people around you. Being stuck in an office all day with someone who has high levels of anxiety, coupled with low self-esteem and a garrulous tongue can be incredibly difficult, due to the emotional quagmire they carry with them and in which they exist. It can suck you in and drag you down. By the same token then, how *you* feel will also impact your family members, friends and colleagues.

If your mood is having a negative impact on someone else, they might begin to avoid you so that they don't have to deal with your emotional residue. A classic sign that loved ones are getting tired of your moods is when they start to suggest you see a counsellor, GP or therapist of some kind. They do this because they feel powerless to help, they are out of their depth and it is a form of self-preservation! Re-directing your mood to a professional, means that they can go back to just being your friend or partner, rather than an emotional safety net, sounding board or dumping ground. Bear in mind that how you feel and how you express those feelings will leave its residue wherever you go. This is as true for positive feelings as it is for negative ones, so if you can, spread joy, love and light.

DEEPER HEALING: OWN YOUR FEELINGS

Your emotions are entirely *your* responsibility. If you are feeling jealous of someone, for instance, there is no point in trying to place the blame for your jealousy onto that individual. It isn't their fault that you are jealous! They are probably just living their life. However, something about them and the life they lead has triggered a jealous reaction in you, so this is something that you need to explore further. *Why* are you envious of them? What do they have that you don't, or what are you secretly afraid of losing? Examining an emotion in this way will help you to discover what your real needs are. Are you envious because someone has published a book? Could that envy be an indication that you are not progressing your own creative dreams with enough dedication, or do you fear that you lack the talent to write a book?

Journalling is the best way to excavate your emotions and get to the bottom of them. Use the prompts below, come up with your own or just start writing and reflecting on your feelings.

- *Why am I experiencing this emotion?*

- *Has it been triggered by a specific person/issue/event?*

- *What are my fears surrounding this person/issue/event?*

- *Do these fears relate to my hopes and dreams for the future?*

- *Have I felt like this before in the past and if so when?*

- *Could this feeling be an emotional hangover from that time?*

- *How do I take responsibility for my feelings regarding this issue?*

- *How do I begin to feel better?*

No-one else can *make* you feel jealous or insecure or whatever. You do that to yourself! You do it by ruminating on the negative feelings and blaming others, rather than making a note of it on an intellectual level and then diving deep into your psyche to discover where it comes from and what it is trying to tell you about yourself. Your emotions are like a text message from your higher self and they are always trying to tell you something. Take responsibility and excavate them to uncover their hidden meanings.

RESPONDING VS. REACTING

A key component of emotional intelligence is being able to respond, rather than react. Reacting is the knee-jerk we mentioned earlier. It is rash and in the moment, a sudden explosion of emotion that might not be either appropriate or proportionate to the situation. Responding on the other hand, takes a bit longer and that is because when you respond, you do so in a very deliberate way, having considered how your response will impact others and what your motivations are for giving it. Reacting is dramatic. Responding is intellectually sophisticated.

Children react all the time. We tend to call it back-chat. One child starts shouting, so the other shouts in return. One child lashes out, so the other hits back. One child sticks out their tongue, so the other child does likewise.

A reaction is usually a direct reflection of the action which provoked it. It is impulsive and is powered by emotion, rather than intellect. Many adults also operate from this same emotional state, because it is all they know. When faced with a situation they don't like, they immediately start to act out their worries, fears and indignation. This reaction is triggered by the current discomfort that they are feeling. One example of reacting would be that of road-rage, where someone loses their temper because of a minor infringement by another motorist. Their behaviour is disproportionate to the event. It is an over-*reaction*.

Responding however, comes from the intellect. It means that you have engaged your brain before speaking! A response is a well-considered and mindful reply, coming from a place of logic. It is strong and assertive and can have a profound impact. It can also be used to diffuse a negative situation, with a calmer approach. It demonstrates wisdom and strategy.

SIMPLE SELF-CARE: TAKE A PAUSE, THEN RESPOND
Whenever you are in a difficult situation you make a personal choice whether to respond or react. This is something that is entirely within your control. If you are in the habit of reacting to things, use this little trick as a reminder to respond instead. Whenever you are feeling fraught, take two or three deep breaths, then pause. Do nothing. Assess the situation (go back to this exercise in Chapter 9), make a quick mental battle plan and respond accordingly. Do you need to walk away, calm someone down or formulate a logical argument before you speak? Whatever you need to do, take another deep breath, then forge ahead with your response.

WITCHY WAYS: BECOME UNSHAKABLE MEDITATION
Meditation is a great way to calm the mind in the midst of trouble
and emotional turmoil. Find a quiet place and sit comfortably.
Close your eyes and regulate your breathing. Now imagine that
you are an unshakable individual, full of inner poise. How do you
stand, how do you speak, how do you interact with others from
this sophisticated emotional state? Visualise yourself handling
tough situations with a calm, quiet authority. When you have a
clear picture of this new, unshakable you, start to repeat the mantra
below.

My inner poise will not be shaken

I respond with mental sophistication

CHAPTER 18

SPIRITUAL SELF-CARE

Religion and spirituality can have a deeply positive effect on your mental wellness. This is because most kinds of spirituality teach forgiveness, letting go of the past, finding peace and calm through meditation, prayer or spell-craft and the belief that something bigger than you is guiding and protecting you. This isn't only true of the main orthodox religions, but can also be applied to less formal types of spirituality as well.

If you don't believe in anything at all then the world is likely to be a very grey place and day to day life will seem quite futile, with no bigger picture to support it. However, having a degree of belief that we are all somehow connected with divinity and with one another, leads to a more compassionate, optimistic and fulfilled life.

For Wiccans, this belief in divinity and interconnectedness comes from nature. The natural world is our church and we spend time out in nature as much as possible, even if that is simply by nurturing our own garden or a collection of potted plants. This connection with the cycle of life, death and rebirth means that we have a sense of continuity and security. The darkest night will always be broken by the first light of dawn. The deepest winter will always be followed by the fresh flush of spring. Life goes on and therefore, so must we.

MAGICAL THINKER

In psychotherapy we frequently refer to the *magical thinker*, which is a part of the psyche that focuses on possibility and how we can influence our own circumstances and life experience. Most pagans have a high degree of magical thinking, because without it, we wouldn't even *try* to cast a spell! Magical thinking is essential in all kinds of spirituality because you are effectively holding a belief in something which cannot be proven. Some people find this easier than others.

Magical thinking includes a deep belief in things like fate, destiny, serendipity, superstition, wishes, dreams and rituals. You are introduced to magical thinking during childhood, when you are told to blow out the candles on your birthday cake or toss a coin into a well while making a wish. This is magical thinking at work, as you visualise your wish as if it has already come true. You were also engaging your magical thinker when you pretended to be Wonder Woman or Superman!

Spell-craft, prayer, law of attraction, cosmic ordering and so on, are all types of magical thinking and they each relate to how you perceive limitation and possibility. When used correctly, magical thinking can be a very powerful tool in its own right. However, there are pitfalls to it and too much magical thinking is actually quite bad for you because it can lead to apathy, passivity, and conditions such as OCD and paranoia.

Positive Magical Thinking

In a positive sense, magical thinking can help you to think in terms of possibility, rather than limitation. This means that you are more likely to start problem solving when faced with an obstacle or set-back of some kind, instead of seeing the obstacle as an immovable limitation, restricting what you can achieve. It is the magical thinker that determines ambitions, goals and achievements for you to aim for. It believes that you *can* succeed, even when the odds are stacked against you. Obviously, a degree of positive magical thinking is essential in achieving any goal, from passing a driving test to graduating from university or getting a promotion at work. You have to believe that these things are possible, in order to achieve them and that is where the magical thinker steps in and shows you a vision of your future. It also develops your sense of being guided and protected by forces outside of yourself.

Negative Magical Thinking

Conversely, a negative aspect to the magical thinker can actually hold you back or derail your life completely. Negative magical thinking means believing in things over which you have entirely no control, such as a lotto win to get you out of financial difficulty or saving yourself for your soul mate, who might never show up. This type of mind-set leads to apathy and passivity in your own life, as you sit and wait for the charmed outcome to come along and rescue you from your reality. Negative magical thinking also involves a heavy degree of superstition which can lead to obsessive compulsive behaviours such as checking and double checking that the oven is off before you leave the house, or excessive hand-washing to avoid germs etc.

SIMPLE SELF-CARE: MONITOR YOUR MAGICAL THINKER

Being able to identify your magical thinking patterns means that you can quickly over-ride any negative aspects to this part of your psyche. If all you do is dream, without taking action on your dreams and ambitions, chances are that you are being governed by negative magical thinking habits. Are you overly superstitious? Can you solve problems as they arise, or do you helplessly wait for outside intervention? Again, this is the kind of magical thinking that will hold you back. Get pro-active and start taking steps to make your goals a reality. Possibility is all around you, but you have to meet it half way! Stop waiting for everything to just come to you, because it won't and you will waste your life in waiting for it.

SPIRITUAL POTTERING AROUND

Have you ever spent an entire afternoon just pottering around? Being busy doing little jobs and small tasks is a very productive way to relax and it should be incorporated into your self-care practice. Pottering isn't only enjoyable, it is beneficial too, because it gets you out of your head and into your body, so it's a valuable way to short-circuit flashbacks, fragmented memories, worrying and so on. In addition, pottering around can give you lots of the *little wins* we talked about earlier, as you accomplish things that might have been on your to-do list for some time, or you tackle those jobs that have been bothering you the most.

Spiritual pottering can be especially relaxing, almost meditative, because you are handling things which have a special and sacred significance to you. Living a magical life involves a certain amount of upkeep and maintenance. You need to make sure that your magical supplies are in good order, so that you can find what you need quickly when you cast. As a form of self-care, spiritual pottering can help you to assess where you are magically, as you note the things you have and what needs to be replenished. This kind of pottering is also a good time to declutter your magical items and books. If there are things that you don't use or which no longer resonate with you, cleanse them and pass them on to someone who will appreciate them more.

SIMPLE SELF-CARE: SPIRITUAL POTTERING TASKS
Set aside an hour or two this week and start pottering. Here are some ideas for how you can spend time indulging in some magical meandering.

- Clean and re-arrange your altar space

- Cleanse your crystals and tools

- Organise your tarot and oracle cards, donating ones you don't use to a friend or to charity

- Make an inventory of your spell supplies and replenish any that are running low

- Pot up some seedlings to make a herb garden

- Organise your dried herbs and throw away any that are out of date

- Make your own candles or soaps

- Organise your magical books and donate those you no longer need

- Make a smudge bundle (see below)

- Perform a magical cleansing in your home to release any stagnant energies

- Make a body scrub and take a cleansing shower (see below)

WITCHY WAYS: MAKE A CALMING LAVENDER BODY SCRUB

Items Required: You will need a mixing bowl, wooden spoon, half a cup of sea salt, almond oil, lavender essential oil, dried lavender, an empty jar and lid.

In a bowl, mix the sea salt with enough almond oil to make a thick paste. Add two or three teaspoons of dried lavender and mix it in thoroughly. Next, add 5-10 drops of lavender oil, depending on how strong you want the fragrance to be and stir it in. Once the paste is thoroughly mixed together, transfer it to the jar and put on the lid. Use as a body scrub next time you shower. As you do so imagine that you are scrubbing away anything that holds you back. Shed the dead skin of trauma and self-doubt and step out of the shower with a magical glow that enables you to take on the world!

WITCHY WAYS: SAGE AND LAVENDER SMUDGE BUNDLES

Items required: enough fresh sage and lavender to create a couple of bundles, natural twine or string

To make your own smudge bundles, harvest enough fresh stems of sage and lavender to make two bundles, each approximately 5cm in diameter. Begin with the sage and make it into a small posy in your hand, adding a stem at a time, then adding stems of lavender on top. Make sure the bundle is as even as possible, then holding it firmly, begin to wrap the string around the bundle, moving from the stems of the herbs to the top and back again so that the string criss-crosses and secures the herbs in place. Tie the string tightly to secure the bundle and hang upside down to dry. Leave in place until all the herbs have dried thoroughly all the way through. To use, light the end of the smudge bundle until it glows red, then blow out the flame and let the bundle smoulder. Gently waft the fragrant smoke around yourself, your home and property, to cleanse the area of all negative energy and bad vibes. When you have finished, stub out the bundle and leave it in an ashtray until you are sure it has been extinguished. Repeat each month as the moon wanes, to keep your space positive and peaceful.

DAILY DEVOTIONALS

Spending time at your altar each day is a great way to ground your energy and to find your spiritual centre. This is especially important when you are going through a difficult time, because the calmness found in devotional activities can help to diffuse any inner turmoil you might be feeling. So what exactly is a daily devotional? Simply put, it is an activity you do to feel closer to the divine, one which usually takes place in a scared space, such as in a church, out in nature or at your altar.

You can incorporate daily devotionals into your schedule at a time that suits you, working it around your job and family commitments. Of course, there will be days when you are too busy to spend time sitting at your altar and that's okay. You might like to do this practice first thing in the morning, to set you up for the day, or you might want to make it a part of your night time routine, with a twilight devotional. Whatever you choose is fine. There is no right or wrong way to do this, but making it a part of your self-care routine will ensure that you make the most of this spiritual form of deep healing.

DEEPER HEALING: DAILY DEVOTIONAL ACTIVITIES
A devotional activity is anything that serves to connect you with your spirituality and chosen path. It is a way of communicating with the divine in order to seek guidance and to better understand yourself. Making time for your spirituality in this way means that you become more grounded and so you are less likely to be buffeted around by the whims of others. You can find your centre whenever you choose, asking for guidance and comfort from your own personal understanding of the divine. Here are some devotional ideas that you might like to add into your spiritual self-care practice.

- Read spiritual books

- Light candles on your altar and sit in quiet contemplation.

- Light a stick of incense at your altar and dedicate it to your chosen deity. Commune with that deity as the incense burns

- Write your own herbal journal, profiling the magical properties of the herbs you use, how you use them and what the results were

- Listen to spiritual music

- Write a poem about your beliefs and experiences

- Sit at your altar and ask an open question, then close your eyes and see what messages and thoughts come up

- Lay out a spread of tarot or oracle cards and conduct a personal reading for yourself

- Write in your Book of Shadows or spiritual journal

- Mix up a blend of magical herbs for a specific purpose

- Perform a blessing cup ritual for someone (see below)

- Invoke a guardian angel or spirit guide (see below)

- Practice gratitude

WITCHY WAYS: A WICCAN BLESSING CUP RITUAL

Have you ever wished that you could help someone who is going through a tough time, but you don't know how? Why not try a Blessing Cup Ritual? Lots of Wiccans like to make use of a Blessing

Cup in their magic to send love and bright blessings to those who need it most. This is a goblet or chalice that is used to store the names of the people you are trying to help by sending positive thoughts and blessings their way. It is a separate vessel from the altar chalice, which is used to hold ritual wine or to represent the element of water.

Your Blessing Cup can be any kind of vessel that you like, plain or decorative, it's up to you. Once you have your vessel, on the night of a full moon, light a stick of Night Queen incense and pass the cup through the smoke several times to cleanse it. Then sprinkle a little spring water onto the cup and say the following incantation to dedicate the cup to its new purpose:

Scared Blessings fill this cup

Blessing the names within

Send magic bright to light them up

Let healing magic begin.

Now, whenever you wish to send magical blessings to someone, wherever they are, simply write their name on a slip of paper, fold it up, kiss it with love and drop it into the Blessing Cup. Leave the names in place until the blessings seem to be manifesting in their lives, then burn the slip of paper with thanks. Keep your Blessing Cup in your scared place, ready to bestow your magic on those who need it most.

WITCHY WAYS: INVOKE A SPIRIT GUIDE

> *Items required: a sage smudge stick, a bell, a white candle and holder*

Timing: perform on the waxing moon

Spirit guides are spiritual helpers who can assist you on your quest for enlightenment. They can be people, elementals, angels or animal totems. You can work with many spirit guides if you want to, but most practitioners work with just one or two. Often they make their presence felt through dreams, or through hints that a certain culture could be of interest to you, leading you to find books, music and documentaries about that culture. We all have spirit guides, but just like angels, they cannot intervene in your life without your permission, so use this simple invocation if you would like to get to know your spirit guide better. First smudge your working area with the sage to cleanse away any negative energy and purify the space. Light the candle and place it in the holder, then ring the bell three times. Now invoke your spirit guide in the following way:

Guiding spirits hear my cry

Send to me my spirit guide

Let me see and let me know

All the wisdom they can show

Guide my steps throughout each day

And teach me to live in a spiritual way

Blessed be

Ring the bell once more and perform any kind of magic or divination practice that you choose. When you are done release the spirit guide with these words and another three rings of the bell to finish:

Blessed Spirit I offer you thanks for being with me

Go if you will, stay if you choose

In love and trust

So mote it be

CHAPTER 19
LIFE SKILLS AND SELF-RELIANCE

Effective self-care should lead to a greater sense of personal power and capability. This in turn, will give you a strong mental and emotional foundation on which to build a collection of practical life-skills and habits that make you increasingly self-reliant such as assertiveness, critical thinking, problem solving, a strong moral compass, decision making and the ability to make sound judgements on your own, without the input of anyone else.

Having a wide skill-set makes you a more well-rounded individual. It can improve your employability, make you a more attractive partner and ensures that you can always stand on your own two feet. We all need a bit of support every now and then, and there is nothing wrong with asking for help when you need it. However, the danger lies in missing the moment when you are ready to get back on your feet, continuing to lean on others for support that you no longer need, but which has become a habit. In psychotherapy, we often refer to this moment as *taking the stabilizers off the bike*. If you'd never had the stabilizers removed from your bicycle when you were a child, you would never have developed competence in riding independently on two wheels. The same is true for coming out of a dark time and learning to live independently again.

WHEN THE DAWN BREAKS

Living through a dark night of the soul means that you have gone through a period of such profound personal growth that everything you thought you knew has been called into question. When such a time hits you, it often strips you of everything that was once familiar, even beloved. All the dead wood of your life is cut away, leaving you raw and vulnerable. This is usually the point where people tend to seek out help, from doctors and therapists.

However, a dark night of the soul isn't meant to be a permanent state of existence. It is a transitional phase and eventually, you are meant to come out at the other side, into a new dawn of understanding. Like any new dawn, this moment begins softly with just a glimmer of light, which spreads across the horizon, bringing in a new day. It can seem all too bright all of a sudden.

You might crave the darkness from which you just came, because it has become familiar to you, as painful as it was. You might be afraid to trust that the light will last. We frequently see this in people who have struggled with addition. After several months of abstinence, they suddenly go back to drinking or using drugs, just at the moment when a new dawn was about to break through in their lives, because the promise of light was too overwhelming for them.

This phase in recovery is when you need to be extra vigilant regarding your self-sabotaging behaviours. You've come a long way on your self-care healing journey, so don't trip yourself up now! Leaning into a new dawn, after a period of trauma or upheaval, can be unsettling. It feels strange to see things from a new perspective. It can make you feel very vulnerable to step into the light where there is nowhere to hide, but it is essential that you do so. You are not meant to live your life in darkness. You are meant to embrace the light and move forward with your life.

SIMPLE SELF-CARE: EMBRACING THE LIGHT
Emergence is a tricky period in any recovery. Like a new butterfly

coming out of the chrysalis, it can be a struggle and it takes a concerted effort to free those wings and fly away. As tempting as it might be to you to remain hidden under the duvet forever, you really must push yourself to get out of your comfort zone and start to build your life up again. Think of something that you used to enjoy doing, before you experienced trauma or low mood, something that you used to enjoy. This could be a sport, a hobby or something else. Make a plan to bring that thing back into your life. See it as a little reward for all that you have endured and take steps to return to this aspect of your old life. This is the beginning of your personal emergence into a brighter future.

BUILDING A SKILL-SET

Having a set of skills works to your advantage because each skill you acquire will improve your overall capability. The more capable you are, the more adaptable you can be when circumstances change without warning, meaning that you can roll with the punches of life more easily. Life skills are vital in any healing journey, regardless of what your ultimate goal might be. Looking for love? Communication skills will be required. Want greater independence? Financial skills will be essential. Need a new job? A driving license can improve your chances of employment.

DEEPER HEALING: HONE YOUR LIFE SKILLS
Building up your skill set will stand you in good stead, no matter what your circumstances are, and it is a great foundation on which to improve your life. Below is a list of life skills which are very valuable indeed, but this is by no means exhaustive. How many of them do you have? How many others can you add?

- Boundary Skills – know how to put up personal boundaries

and how to protect them when someone oversteps the mark.

- Communication Skills – especially listening skills! Vital for all interactions.

- Conflict Resolution & De-Escalation Skills – essential to achieve a win-win result or to calm a volatile situation. Knowing how to pick your battles is important.

- Culinary Skills – knowing how to cook healthy meals from scratch, baking and so on, means that you know exactly what you are eating and feeding your family.

- Debating Skills – great for getting your point across, politely and without conflict.

- Domestic Skills – knowing how to run and maintain a secure and comfortable home.

- Driving Skills – increases independence and improves job prospects. Everyone needs a getaway car at times!

- Financial Skills– understanding how credit works, create savings and how to budget your income can keep you out of unmanageable debt.

- First Aid Skills – vital if you have kids or care for someone, though useful for everyone to have as you never know when you might need this knowledge.

- Foreign Language Skills – improves job prospects and opens doors to travel or working abroad.

- Home Remedy Skills – prevent visits to the doctor and

saves on prescription charges for common ailments such
as coughs, colds and minor ailments.

- Navigation Skills – essential if you want to travel alone.
  Don't rely on sat-nav!

- Risk Assessment Skills – vital for self-preservation,
  especially in unfamiliar territory.

- Self-Awareness & Self-Soothing – know your triggers, your
  moods, your issues and have the ability to sooth yourself
  and take back control when they rear their ugly heads.

- Self-Defence Skills – great for confidence, feelings of safety,
  useful to have just in case.

- Social Media Skills – understand how it can be used against
  you, so you can protect yourself accordingly. Know how
  to make the most of its benefits.

- Spiritual Skills – meditation, prayer, communing with
  divinity etc. are all useful for comfort, belief and existential
  explorations.

- Technology Skills – you don't need to be a whizz-kid, but
  you do need the basics.

These are just some of the life skills that can help to stack the
advantages in your favour, especially when job hunting or seeking
to make a major life change. Of course, you probably won't have
all these skills in place right now, but I hope that the list serves
to inspire you, because the more skills you have, the more of a
well-rounded, self-sufficient person you will become.

DEEPER HEALING: DE-ESCALATION SKILLS

Knowing how to diffuse a situation or calming areas of potential conflict means that you are less likely to get drawn into unpleasant interactions that quickly get out of hand or become dangerous. Often, people will demonstrate anger and aggression when really they are upset, frightened or deeply worried about something. They project anger to hide their vulnerability with a temporary show of superficial strength. Bear this in mind the next time someone is angry with you and see if you can get to the emotional root of the issue, using these skills.

- Move to a neutral zone.

- Listen carefully to what someone is saying. Endure their tirade with as much grace as possible. They are angry for a reason. Let them express that emotion without interruption, or you will never get to the root emotion that is hidden behind their anger.

- Show that you are listening to them, by nodding and maintaining eye contact.

- Empathise with their situation and try to see it from their perspective. Speak slowly and softly. Show compassion and remember *noblesse oblige*.

- Take ownership and responsibility for *helping* them to fix the issue. Note that you are not offering to fix it for them, only to help them to fix it.

- Work together to come up with a plan to fix things. Decide who will do what and follow through with action.

WITCHY WAYS: WARRIOR PLAITS

There might be times when you know that you are going into situations where conflict is highly possible. If you work in any kind of customer services role, for instance, then it is likely that you will have to face the odd disgruntled and angry client. The same is true for anyone who works in a high stakes environment, such as the NHS or the welfare system. When people are worried about keeping body and soul together, they naturally become very volatile.

The following spell is designed to give you a magical edge when you are heading into conflict. It is a type of knot magic which uses your hair as a tag-lock to connect the spell to you all day. Ideally it requires the practitioner to have hair long enough to make a plait, but as an alternative, you could make a braid from ribbon and wear this on your wrist or carry it in your pocket.

Hair magic was popular with the Vikings, Celts and Gall-Gaidheal and both the men and women wore braids in their hair. Warrior braids served two purposes – first they kept the hair off the face, enabling the warrior to see his enemy, and secondly they carried protection magic within them. You can incorporate warrior braids into your self-care by plaiting your hair with a peaceful intention. Take a section of hair and make a simple three-strand braid, saying the chant below as you plait.

Warrior plaits now woven tight

In twisted braid this spell takes flight

Protection within is deeply bound

Bypass conflict, let peace be found

So mote it be

A LOW-CONFLICT, HIGH-PEACE LIFE

It goes without saying that a life of peace and calm is better for your mental health than one of constant conflict. Conflict increases stress and stress is the gateway to other mental health issues. Increasing your autonomy, along with your ability to deal with conflict in a positive way, ensures that you can reduce the amount of stress you hold on to. Living a high-peace life is always possible, no matter how much conflict you have faced in the past. Peace is always an option, but you do have to make the conscious decision to choose it as your path going forward. But what do you do if the very *idea* of conflict stresses you out? Try carrying a worry stone to help alleviate your anxiety.

WITCHY WAYS: EMPOWER A WORRY STONE

Worry stones are a very popular witches tool. They can be used to absorb negative energy, such as worry, anxiety, stress etc. You will need a stone of some kind. This could be a pebble that you found on a beach or riverbed or a crystal tumble stone. The stone should be one that you find pleasing and which is comfortable to hold in your hand and carry with you. Once you have found the right stone, leave it in the light of the moon for a full lunar cycle, from new moon to new moon. Let it soak up the energies of the lunar light. Once your stone has been empowered by the moon, carry it with you and use it as a worry stone to help calm your fears of conflict, by holding it in your hand and rubbing your thumb across it. This repetitive, soothing motion helps to calm the nerves.

INTELLECTUAL NAPS

In the midst of turmoil, sometimes all your mind needs, is a little nap. Napping has been proven to improve brain function and memory. It helps you to de-stress and can facilitate problem solving, hence the phrase *sleep on it*. In addition, taking a nap can increase your mental capacity to learn new things and helps the brain to retain information. Yet people still feel guilty for getting a little shut eye in the middle of the afternoon!

Society seems to condition us to believe that if the sun is up, we should be wide awake and fully alert at all times, but this isn't always beneficial. The truth is, having a brief 30-minute nap is good for you, and there are times when you really need the extra sleep. Bereavement is known to increase tiredness, so napping through the grief is essential. Illness obviously dictates that you should sleep more, as that is when your body heals best, and napping in your senior years can help to ward off dementia and age-related forgetfulness.

Furthermore, some of the brightest brains in history, such as Leonardo da Vinci, Napoleon Bonaparte, Albert Einstein and Winston Churchill, all took regular naps in the middle of the day, to help them think, invent and strategize, so we shouldn't discount napping, for it is a beneficial self-care tool. You could do worse than take a leaf out of their book. You too might have an epiphany as you dream!

SIMPLE SELF-CARE: CREATE A NAP NOOK
Napping should have its own designated space, and while it is possible to nap in bed, this could disrupt your nocturnal sleep pattern. Instead, try to set up a specific place to enjoy your naps. You could curl up in a comfy armchair, stretch out on the couch, recline on a chaise longue, pile cushions on the floor before the fire and drift off for a mid-winter reverie, or lay a blanket out in the garden and slumber to the gentle hum of bumble bees and birdsong. Wherever you choose to nap, make it comfortable and as cosy as possible. Grab a hot water bottle, or your pet, snuggle down and get some shut eye, knowing that you are actually working very hard on improving your mental agility and brain

power. They don't call it a power nap for nothing, so take one today and call it personal research into cognitive functioning! Sweet dreams.

CHAPTER 20
LETTING GO OF THE PAST

Moving forward in your life in a positive way involves letting go of the past. Of course, this is easier said than done, as the things which hurt us often leave deep scars and emotional wounds that take time to heal. Holding on to the past, however, can colour your future in a negative way, because it makes you see the world through *morose-tinted* glasses! It can be hard to move on from the fact that you might have been hurt, injured, betrayed, sabotaged or whatever. But letting go and moving on is the final part of the healing journey. It is what seals the wound. In this chapter then, we are going to explore ways in which you can let go of your past, once and for all. Letting go isn't about unconditional forgiveness. It is about giving yourself a clean slate on which to write out your own future.

FORGIVE AND FORGET?

Whenever people discuss letting go of the past, often the words *forgive and forget* will come up, time and time again. It's one of those platitudes that is easy to say, but not so easy to do in practice. It can even feel quite insulting, depending on what you are being expected to forgive. While it's true that forgiveness has its place in the emergence stage of self-care, it is also true that some things often feel unforgivable. Child abuse, sexual assault, extreme violence etc., are all much harder to forgive than other misdemeanours, because there is a violation of trust involved. In the long term though, holding onto resentment and bitterness will only harm *you*, not the perpetrator, and it can lead to a victim mentality. It is also true that you might never forget the transgressions against you, especially if they have been life-changing. The most important thing is that you do not allow the past to shape your future in a negative way, but you can use it as fuel for motivation.

ANGER AS FUEL

Anger is a very powerful emotion. It holds a lot of energy. That is why you feel like you're going to explode when you are about to lose your temper. Typically, anger swirls around like a ball of fire in the chest cavity. We release it with harsh words, tears and tantrums, sometimes with physical violence, but there are far more positive ways to use the energy that anger supplies you with.

You can use it in the gym to fire you up for a workout routine, or in sports where you have an opponent to compete against. Men tend to do this more naturally than women, as gender conditioning has taught women that it isn't very nice to get angry, or to express it in any way. Feeling angry all the time leads to aggressive interactions and a bad attitude, so if you are frequently accused of these traits then it is highly likely that you are holding onto some repressed anger of some sort. It is a sign that something is eating away at you inside.

Instead of seeing your anger as a bad thing that you must either repress or get rid of, learn to recognise it as the rocket fuel it is. It can empower you if you let it, so use it as a driving force. Thinking of your enemy, as you work to achieve a goal, can be very motivating. If you don't believe this, just try visualising your enemy achieving *your* goal, enjoying the success that follows, instead of you! It's one thing to let go of your enemies, but it's quite another to imagine them achieving all the dreams you hold for yourself!

SIMPLE SELF-CARE: USE ANGER AS FUEL
Releasing your anger in a positive way can improve your motivation and sense of accomplishment. In addition, it leaves you feeling much calmer than before, because you have channelled that energy in a progressive way. It can be the force which gets you out of bed in the morning when nothing else will. It can push you to better yourself. Here then are a few suggestions for how you can use your anger as rocket fuel.

- Use it to spark a positive change in your life.

- Allow anger to energise your body and get moving more productively. No more pacing back and forth, do some real exercise instead.

- Channel anger into a creative project of some kind – write a song, a poem or choreograph an expressive dance.

- Let anger increase your enthusiasm for exercise.

- Release it in a self-defence class, making yourself stronger and safer.

- Play music and dance it out.

- Build your anger into more effective personal boundaries, by telling yourself *Never again will I allow… to happen to me.*

- Use your anger to give the bathroom a good scrub – or the whole house!

- Channel anger into greater determination and perseverance, let it be a progressive emotion.

- Visualise your enemy seeing your success, knowing that they failed to hold you back or tear you down.

- Visualise yourself at your most successful, the last one standing.

SHAME ON YOU!

If anger is like rocket fuel, then shame is an anchor that weighs you down. It will hold you firmly in the past, tethering you to it with an increasingly complex network of knots in your stomach. Furthermore, you will have to carry the weight of that anchor around with you, every day, until you free yourself from the feeling of shame. Often shame is associated with a sense of dishonour or degradation – either you have *been* dishonoured or degraded, or you have *done* something dishonourable or degrading. This lingers in the psyche as shame.

Certain types of trauma are inextricably linked with feelings of shame. Survivor remorse, sexual abuse, domestic violence, abuse in childhood, financial troubles and so on, can all contribute to a deep feeling of shame. Overcoming this emotion is an ongoing process, as sudden shame might creep up on you unawares. The trick is to separate who you are, from what you did, or what was done to you. In this way, it stops being a part of your personal identity and instead is merely an event from the past, one which you overcame and lived to tell the tale. You can also cast the following spell to release lingering feelings of shame.

WITCHY WAYS: RITUAL TO FREE YOURSELF FROM SHAME

> *Items required: a leaf*

> *Timing: perform at full to dark moon*

Go for a walk by a river or stream. As you walk, look for a fallen leaf or flower blossom. When you see one you like, pick it up and silently name it for the type of shame you want to release. When you feel ready, drop the leaf into the river and watch the water carry it away from you. Walk away from the river and don't look back – know that the leaf has gone and is no longer any part of your life. The shame should soon follow it. Repeat the ritual as necessary.

OWN YOUR TRIGGERS!

Just like your emotions, your triggers are also your own responsibility. What does that mean exactly? It means that, although the traumatic event which gave you an overactive trigger response, wasn't usually something that you chose, the triggers that resulted from it are part of your own personal psyche. They are an *internal reaction* to external events. This effectively means that nothing and no-one has the power to *trigger* you – it is your own mind that triggers you. It comes from an internal place and as such it is within your capability to control.

As you work on healing old wounds via self-care, as you have been doing throughout the course of this book, you will begin to feel much less triggered. This is because it is your wounds which smart due to an external influence, but that influence isn't what inflicted the wound. It simply reopened it for a time and reminded you of an old pain. The more healing work you do, the fewer open wounds you will have to be triggered.

DEEPER HEALING: DE-ACTIVATING TRIGGERS
Taking control of your triggers is about recognising the influences
that activate them, so that you can have a deeper understanding
of where the trigger originated. This point of origin is where the
wound lies, and what needs to be addressed, not the external events.
In your notebook, reflect on the following points.

- What are the top three influences or events that trigger
  you? Is it criticism, loud noises, crowds of people, a certain
  place or smell? What are the main three things that trigger
  you over and over again?

- What is it about these things that sets you off and how do
  you react when triggered? Do you get angry or emotional?
  Do you freeze or retreat? Or something else?

- What aspect of your past do these triggers represent? This
  is the point of origin.

- Have you taken steps to address this point of origin, say
  in counselling, or not? If not, why not? Can you take
  action now on getting help to overcome this trigger?

- Bring your mind back to the here and now. Remind yourself
  that whatever happened is in the past and can no longer
  hurt you. Only the residue of that event can hurt you if
  you let it and residue can be cleaned up!

- Whenever you feel triggered in future, remind yourself
  that you are acting out your past, not your present and
  redress this imbalance.

TOUGH-LOVE YOURSELF

In any self-care book there is usually a section about loving yourself. We all know that self-love is the first step towards finding loving relationships, but we rarely talk about how the concept of tough love can be applied in a self-love scenario. Tough love is when you take a firm stance with someone, ignoring their excuses and telling them what needs to happen. It involves lots of straight talking, several home truths and pointing out the behaviours that make someone their own worst enemy.

Tough love can be just as difficult and unpleasant to deliver as it is to receive, because it is a type of intervention and interventions are usually stressful. An intervention is an orchestrated manoeuvre that is designed to bring someone to their senses. In a way, it could be viewed as a positive coercion, because it is done in order to bring about the best outcome for a particular individual, even though they might not be 100% on board with the plan!

DEEPER HEALING: TOUGH-LOVE YOURSELF
How does tough love fit into self-care? Well, if you can learn to tough-love yourself, then you can make a quick intervention of any negative habits, behaviours and excuses you are falling back on. Tough-loving yourself means that *you* don't let *you* get away with anything! You don't make excuses: you make plans which you follow through. You don't ring in sick when you feel lazy: you go to work. You maintain high standards, rather than letting things slip. You take personal responsibility for your thoughts, words and deeds. No excuses. No *Yes, but.* No, *but.* No self-deception. You are honest in your communications with yourself. You know the issues you struggle with, what your sabotaging habits are and you take steps to overcome them. Tough-loving yourself is a form of self-parenting and it is one of the key tools used in the emergence phase of self-care and deep healing. It is holding yourself accountable.

DON'T BE AN ASK-HOLE!

Is it possible to ask too many questions? That depends. Generally speaking, asking questions is a good thing, providing you are willing to listen carefully to the response. If you don't understand something, then it is smart to ask for clarification. However, there are some people who ask nothing but questions and who also do not give anyone a chance to respond, they simply move straight on to the next question. This effectively means that they bombard people with endless questions, while not listening to the reply. They may frequently interrupt with phases such as *Yes, but...No, but...What about...?* It is a road block to conversation, because they are only concerned with getting as many questions out there as possible, but they tend not to be interested in the answers, meaning that there is never a resolution to the issue, only an endless barrage of questions. We sometimes refer to such people as ask-holes!

There are two main psychological reasons why someone might behave this way. The first is that they need a constant feed of reassurance, which they get by asking lots of questions about a particular issue. The second is that they feel the need to appear superior, by asking as many questions as possible in the hopes that they will find one you can't answer! This validates their theory that they know more than you do. Both traits are annoying and an ineffective way of communicating.

SIMPLE SELF-CARE: USE QUESTIONS WITH CARE
When people are frightened or worried, they might try to mask their fear by gleaning as much information as possible, hence they tend to ask too many questions, without being in the frame of mind to take in that new information. When you have concerns about something and you want to find out more, use your questions with care and consideration. And if you've never met a question-mark you didn't love, the tips overleaf might help.

- Try to frame your main concerns into two or three key questions, making sure that these three queries cover all the bases of your issue.

- Ask the questions in a logical order, in a kindly way.

- Give your interviewee time to respond – don't expect an instant answer. You might have had hours or even days to consider your line of questioning, they are hearing your queries for the first time. Give them a chance to gather their intelligence. They might need to speak to someone else, or look something up before they can answer your questions fully. Allow them the time to do this.

- Listen carefully to their reply. Do not interrupt. Do not ask any more questions until you have received and processed the reply to the first question. Make notes if you need to.

- Reflect on the replies you have been given and allow your brain the time it needs to process this new information, before you go in with any further questions.

CHAPTER 21
THE DOOR IS ALWAYS OPEN

Coming through a dark night of the soul, or a period of low mood, can feel like springtime. Suddenly you see bright colours, whereas before everything seemed very grey. You begin to appreciate the little things once more, such as the sound of birdsong, a frosty morning, the sun on your face or a scattering of wild flowers. You become increasingly aware of the gift of your life and more inclined to make the most of it. Suddenly, you want to do *everything*! The world is full of possibility and you are open to it once more. Having finally emerged from the chrysalis, you are ready to test your wings and fly!

This can be a very exciting phase of recovery and healing. It generally means that you are through the worst of it, however, you do still need to pace yourself. Remember that self-care is an ongoing process, so don't stop using these techniques just because you are feeling better. Maintain any self-care routines that you have created and keep building self-care practices into your day regularly, in order to maintain all the benefits. At this stage in the healing process it can be all too easy to become complacent. Don't be, because there are still one or two pitfalls for you to watch out for.

TEMPTATION

Temptation is a very powerful thing. It draws you in and seduces you with promises of *just one sip, just one kiss, just one taste*. But once is never enough, as anyone who has fallen under the spell of a romantic infatuation knows. Once will never be enough and the temptation only grows stronger, the more you dance with the devil of your desires.

Temptation is the deep urge to follow your baser instincts, against the better judgement of your intellect. Usually, temptation leads you to do something that you know to be wrong, or unhealthy, or bad for you, but which feels so good in the moment you just can't help yourself. It entices you to prioritise short term gratification over long term gain. Temptation pulls you like a magnate in the wrong direction. It is deeply alluring, mesmerizing and enticing.

Everyone experiences temptation at some time or other, although it can often take you completely by surprise, seeming to come out of nowhere, dropping out of the clear blue sky. It is a strong and vital force of nature, for without temptation we would never form romantic relationships or start families. Temptation drives procreation, so it is a force to be reckoned with. When it is working against you though, tempting you to light a cigarette or have one more glass of wine, it can be a very destructive force indeed, sending you straight back to square one, if you are not careful. Temptation, like any other toxic substance, needs to be handled with care.

DEEPER HEALING: RESISTING TEMPTATION

Learning how to resist temptation, and resist it consistently, is an essential part of your self-care because without this resistance, you are likely to fall back into old coping mechanisms when life gets tough again, even if those coping strategies were harmful. Self-control and will-power will help to keep temptation at bay. Try using the following techniques for resisting your personal temptations.

- The first step to resistance, is to remove yourself from temptation's path. Whether the temptation is a person, an old habit, an addiction or whatever – remove yourself from the places you would normally encounter it. This includes social media.

- Spend time with people who understand the temptation and who can help steer you away from it, lending their wise guidance to your own will-power. This could be a trusted family member, a friend or a more formal support group. When you feel the pull of temptation, reach out to this positive source of support for moral assistance.

- Distract yourself. Do something completely unrelated to your temptation. Go for a walk, read a book, watch a film, do a crossword puzzle. Keep yourself busy in other ways, until the urge to give in to temptation has reduced.

- Change your associations of the temptation, so instead of saying *Wow, he's so hot!* Say instead, *I bet his feet stink. Glad I'm not washing his socks!*

- Be honest with yourself and others. Admitting that you are tempted by something, is not the same as giving into that temptation. It also gives other people a chance to support you in your resistance.

- Envision what the consequences of giving into temptation might be. Will it retrigger a negative habit or an addiction, will it leave you feeling used and alone or resentful? What will this *cost* you in the long run and is it really worth the risk? Temptation usually comes with a heavy price tag.

- Try to anticipate when you are emotionally weakened and therefore more vulnerable to temptation. This could be when you have had some bad news and you are tempted to reach out to the wrong person for support, or when you feel down in the dumps and decide to have a few drinks with friends. Identify how your mood changes your resistance to temptation.

- Reinforce your resistance with a touch of magic...

WITCHY WAYS: A SPELL TO RESIST TEMPTATION

> *Items required: a cauldron or heatproof bowl, note paper, a black pen, athame or carving tool, a symbol of the temptation, a black candle and holder, lighter*
>
> *Timing: perform on the full to waning moon*

Take the items to a quiet place where you will not be disturbed. Carve your name or initials down the length of the black candle, then carve a keyword that represents your personal temptation on the other side. Place the candle in a holder and put the object that represents the temptation in front of it. Light the candle, then write the nature of the temptation at the top of a sheet of note paper, followed by the incantation below:

> *Trick or treat?*
>
> *I will not cheat*
>
> *To my values I stay true*
>
> *Alarm bells ring*
>
> *Moral compass swings*
>
> *I resolve my resistance anew*
>
> *So mote it be.*

Say this charm thrice, then fold the paper three times, light it in the candle and allow it to burn in the cauldron. Let the candle burn out naturally, as it burns the temptation out of your heart. Repeat the spell as often as needed. Each time you resist, you are galvanising your own moral compass and your long term success. Be proud of yourself for saying no.

FEAR IS ALWAYS MAGNIFIED

We all have a tendency to magnify our internal fears. In extreme cases, this results in high anxiety and catastrophizing, but we all magnify our fears to some extent. This is because fear is based in the unknown and it makes you defensive. Even good things can make you fearful. Lots of people fear success, for instance, and take self-sabotaging steps to avoid it! You might fear what your life will be like without the crutch of an addiction, or a partner, or a particular job. You might have fears regarding moving forward, because you're not sure what the future holds for you. All of this is natural.

It is perfectly normal to be apprehensive about any change in circumstances, even the positive ones. As you emerge on your healing journey, you might become fearful of meeting someone new and the disruption a new relationship will cause to your day to day life. Love is always unexpected, yet we have to make space for it if we want it to stick around, and that can be a scary prospect. The same is true for a new career path, or a new baby. Every time something new comes into your life, you will need to adjust and adapt to the shape of it. You will need to get comfortable with the idea of it, before you are happy to let it in completely and make the necessary adjustments it demands of you. Fortunately, this is where visualisation can help you.

WITCHY WAYS: VISUALISE YOUR FUTURE
There is a saying which goes something along the lines of: *If you*

cannot dream it, you cannot become it. Simply put, this means that you need to be able to see the future you want to enjoy. If you want new romance, a family, a great career, a wonderful holiday – you need to be able to envision yourself experiencing those things. Visualisation allows you to do just that. It is a kind of focused day-dreaming, that helps your mind to become comfortable with things that are currently outside of your experience. It's a way of training yourself to receive, so that when all those good things come to you, your fear of the changes they bring about, will have been minimised. All you have to do is sit in quiet contemplation and imagine the life that you want to live. Make a soothing cup of tea and just ponder on what you want to attract and manifest in your life over the next year or so. See yourself living that life and feel the joy that it will bring. Do this visualisation exercise every day if possible, to train your brain to get comfortable with things that feel aspirational to you now.

SET-BACKS AND BACK-SLIDES

Life can be very unpredictable at times. Just because you are healing and keeping on top of your self-care doesn't mean that you will never experience a set-back. Jobs can be lost, relationships end, friendships turn sour and finances can be a bit up and down. In fact, life often throws a spanner in the works just when you think things are going well and you are about to achieve a big goal. It seems unfair and it can feel like an attack, but it's really not personal. You didn't do anything wrong. It's just part of the process. This is how your resilience, bounce-back and problem solving abilities are honed.

Sometimes a set-back is actually a blessing in disguise. It could be that you didn't get that job because the company is actually in financial trouble and about to go under. It could be that your hot new date didn't show up because he was being arrested for a misdemeanour, or interrogated by the wife you didn't know he had! Such lucky escapes mean that the universe is actually protecting you.

Witches believe that there is a reason for everything and that includes the set-backs too. When something unexpected happens to derail your plans, it is usually because you were on the wrong path and something even better is coming along. A set-back frequently turns out to be a set-up, in that life is redirecting you to something else which will prove to be even more beneficial to you. You might lose your magazine column, but gain a book deal. Or lose a local job, just to be offered one in your dream location. Such things do happen, so try to have patience when it feels like you are being held back from an opportunity, as an even bigger opportunity is usually waiting in the wings.

Back-slides are also quite natural, though these are usually self-directed rather than as a result of unexpected events. A back-slide tends to happen shortly after you've had some kind of break-through. It could be that things are going so well, you become complacent and stop putting as much effort into your goals and self-healing, leading to a temporary pause on your progress. Suddenly your optimism fades away, you pick up old habits again, you fail an exam or you find yourself back in a rut. This is life's little way of cracking the whip and telling you to keep putting the effort in! It's okay to have down time, but don't allow yourself to backslide for too long. If you do, you might find that one aspect of self-healing which you thought you had nailed down, suddenly requires your attention again. If that happens, go back to basics, work on fulfilling those needs and then press ahead. Bear in mind that progress is never linear, it has its peaks and troughs.

THE CRYING GAME

I once told a little boy who came to see me when his mother was very sick, that when he cried, he was really just watering his courage, making space inside for it to grow, and it's absolutely true. Tears are one of the ways in which the body processes emotion. Holding back your tears means that you are not giving yourself a chance to grow into greater strength. Crying is good for you! Whether it's a silvery stream of silent tears, or heart wrenching sobs, regardless of if you are weeping or wailing, expressing sorrow through a good cry is beneficial. Don't ever apologise for your tears. Don't ever hold them back. Release them, because crying is not a sign of weakness, it is the path to future fortitude, so cry whenever you need to.

INVITE JOY INTO YOUR LIFE

Have you ever invited joy into your life? Or love, excitement, happiness, miracles? If you haven't then it is time that you began! This is a personal trick of mine that I use whenever I'm feeling a little down in the dumps or sad and it has always worked to bring something to me that is guaranteed to put a smile on my face. I share it with you now, with lots of love and many blessings.

SIMPLE SELF-CARE: MIRACLES ARE COMING IN TO LAND!
You don't technically need any tools for this ritual, but you can light a candle or incense if you want to. You are going to speak your wish directly to the universe, so close your eyes and think about how you are feeling right now – sad, lonely, fearful, anxious etc. It's okay to have these feelings. Know that they will pass. Next say out loud

Miracles are coming in to land in my life!

The runway is clear: they have permission to land.

Miracles are coming in to land in my life!

Gifts I can hold in my heart, head and hands.

So mote it be.

Keep saying this until it feels true. Repeat *Miracles are coming in to land in my life* as a mantra, whenever you are overwhelmed by darker emotions. Within a month, something will happen to make you gleeful, because you have proactively invited joy into your life.

SIMPLE SELF-CARE: SEND OUT SMILES AND MIRACLES
Asking for miracles to land in your life is really only half the story. It is just as important to actively send out miracles to others too, so that you make someone else smile. Small, unexpected acts of kindness work well to brighten anyone's day. Think of something you could do to make someone smile this week. Here are some ideas:

- Pay for the person behind you in a coffee shop

- Send someone a bunch of flowers

- Send someone a letter or hand written card

- Make a comfort scarf for someone and give it to them as a surprise

- Bake something for someone

- Cast protection spells for the Armed Forces

- Cast protection spells for the Emergency Services

- Give someone a lift in your car

- Drop in on an elderly neighbour for a chat

- Donate to a favourite charity

- Volunteer with a charity

- Leave treat bags of sweeties, with notes from the fairies, in a playground for children to find

- Feed a stray cat – but make sure it is a stray before you encourage it!

- Buy food for a homeless person

THE DOOR IS ALWAYS OPEN

In the world of psychotherapy, we often tell clients that our door is always open, meaning that they can always come back into therapy at any time if they find that they are struggling. Progress isn't linear, meltdowns are normal and challenges are inevitable. As this book doesn't have a door, I have instead compiled a list of UK contacts and resources for your information. I hope that you will never have need of these services, but know that one-to-one assistance is available if you do. All of these charitable services are free. It's okay to ask for help.

Crisis – for homelessness – www.crisis.org.uk

Cruse Bereavement Care – for bereavement – 0808 808 1677 www.cruse.org.uk

GamCare – for gambling issues – 0808 8020 133 www.gamcare. org.uk

Mind – for mental health crisis – www.mind.org.uk

Refuge – for domestic violence – 0808 2000 247 refuge.org.uk

Step-Change – for debt issues – www.stepchange.org

The Samaritans – for general support – 116 123 www.samaritans. org

Turning Point – for alcoholism and drug addiction – www. turning-point.co.uk

CONCLUSION
CHECKING OUT...

As we come to the end of our self-care journey together, I hope that you have found the methodology in these pages useful. The greatest act of magic you will ever perform is the alchemy of your mind, turning baseness into boldness, darkness into light and misery to joy. Writing this book has certainly been a joyful process for me. It has given me the opportunity to share more of what I know in terms of psychology and psychotherapy, based on my training and experience as a therapist, in the hopes that it will reach the people who need it most and help them to turn their life around. Positive change is always possible. There are no lost causes.

The magic contained within these pages is subtle, yet deeply profound and life changing. Use these skills to better your life, to improve your mental agility and to build your resilience, so that you can step up in the face of life's challenges, rather than stepping back. Life gets very difficult at times, for everyone. May this book and the self-care teachings within it, give you the light you need to overcome even the darkest of shadows. You have everything you need inside you – strength, courage, wisdom, love, joy, hope, fortitude and robustness – all you have to do is set those things free. Let them guide and protect you.

It's time to take the stabilizers off the bike. It's time to test your wings and see how high you can fly. Know that whoever and wherever you are, I am always rooting for you to succeed and achieve all that your heart desires. Farewell, my magical reader, until our next merry meeting and may the brightest of miracles come in to land in your life!

Serene blessings,

Marie Bruce x

INDEX

ACKNOWLEDGEMENTS

This book is the culmination of over thirty years' experience as a practicing witch, coupled with five years' university level training and subsequent experience as a qualified psychotherapist. There have been several people along the way who have supported and influenced me, not least of which is my mother, Jaqueline Weatherill, who always has my back when things get tough. I couldn't have got through the training without you, Mum, so thank you for your endless support and sensible pep-talks when I felt like dropping out of the course! You were right, it was worth it in the end.

I am deeply indebted to my psychotherapy tutors at *Sheffield City College*, especially Millie Anderson, whose lessons were always fun and informative. You never put too much pressure on us Millie, but somehow you managed to bring out the best in each of us as individuals. You are one teacher that I will never forget, for all the right reasons. The same goes to the ›other students who went through all the various levels of training with me and who are now fellow counsellors, in particular Joanne Bacon, Jo Gregory, Louise Crofts, Sara Shardlow, Stephanie Newman, Lisa Tindle-Godley, Heather Davison, Tracy Scott, Josie Smith, Maryam Mahmud and Rowan Bell – thanks for understanding my sarcastic humour and finding it witty and amusing. It was a pleasure to be in the clique with you all! In addition, I owe a huge thank you to the team at *Cruse Bereavement Care Sheffield*, especially Lee Adams, my clinical practice supervisor, who gave me a shoulder to cry on when the tales of trauma and woe, all got a bit too much for me, and also Mary Watton our receptionist, for her calm, nurturing presence and the never-ending supply of tea and biscuits. A special mention has to go to Dr. Ted Turner, for allowing me to glean from his super-posh Cambridge education every time we meet! I enjoy our patient/doctor domestics because you always make me see things in a different light. You're one of my favourite sparring partners! I hope that I have done you all proud with the healing, psychotherapy aspects of this book.

Last but not least, I want to give a big shout out to all my friends in uniform: in the South Yorkshire Police Force and in the military, both Veteran and those currently serving in the British Army, the RAF and The Red Arrows. This book would not be what it is without your inspirational, motivational influence in my life. Some of you were deployed as I wrote this book, but I want you to know that you are never out of my thoughts, or my protection. I am so proud to call you my friends and to surround you all with as much protection magic as I can conjure. There is room on my broom for all of you!

Love to you all,

Marie xxx

FURTHER READING

Books by the same author

Wicca

Celtic Spells

Moon Magic Book and Card Deck

The Book of Spells

Green Witchcraft

Wicca for Self-Transformation

Moon Magic

Celtic Magic Book and Card Deck

Glamour Magic

Books on Psychotherapy

MCLEOD, John (1993). An Introduction to Counselling, Berkshire, Open University Press.
MILNE, Aileen (1999). Understanding Counselling, London, Hodder Headline

SANDERS, Pete (2011). First Steps in Counselling, 4th ed.,
    Ross-on-Wye, PCCS Books
STEWART, Ian (2014). Transactional Analysis Counselling in
    Action 4th ed,. London, SAGE Publications.

Books on Witchcraft

Buckland, Raymond, *Buckland's Complete Book of Witchcraft*,
    Llewellyn 1997, 0875420508
Cunningham, Scott, *Wicca: A Guide for the Solitary
    Practitioner*, Llewellyn 1997, 0875421180
Cunningham, Scott, *Living Wicca: A Further Guide for the
    Solitary Practitioner*, Llewellyn. 1997, 0875421849
Cunningham, Scott, *The Truth About Witchcraft Today*,
    Llewellyn, 1997, 087542127X
Curott, Phyllis, *Book of Shadows*, Piatkus, 1998, 0749918594
Davis, Owen, *The Oxford Illustrated History of Witchcraft &
        Magic*, Oxford University Press, 2017, 9780199608447
De Pulford, Nicola, *Spells & Charms*, Godsfield Press,
    1999,   189943464X
Greenleaf, Cerridwen, *The Practical Witch's Spellbook*,
    Running Press, 2018, 9780762493203
Guiley, Rosemary Ellen, *The Encyclopaedia of Witches and
    Witchcraft*, Facts on File LTD, 1989, 0816022682
Horne, Fiona, *Witch: A Magical Journey*, *A Guide to Modern
    Witchcraft*, Thorsons Harper Collins, 2000, 0007103999
Hutton, Ronald, *The Triumph of the Moon: A History of
    Modern Pagan Witchcraft*, Oxford University Press, 1999,
    0198207441
Illes, Judika, *The Element Encyclopaedia of Witchcraft*, Element
    Harper Collins, 2005, 0007192932
Illes, Judika, *The Element Encyclopaedia of 5000 Spells*, Element
    Harper Collins, 2004, 0007164653
Kane, Aurora, *Moon Magic*, Quarto Publishing Group, 2020,

9781577151876

Jordan, Michael, *Witches: An Encyclopedia of Paganism and Magic*, Kyle Cathie Limited, 1998, 1856263053

Moorey, Teresa, *Spells & Rituals*, Hodder & Stoughton, 1999, 0340730625

Moorey, Teresa, *Witchcraft: A Beginner's Guide*, Hodder & Stoughton, 1996, 0340670142

Moorey, Teresa, *Witchcraft: A Complete Guide*, Hodder & Stoughton, 2000, 0340753242

Morningstar, Sally, *The Wicca Pack: Weaving Magic into your Life*, Godsfield Press, 2001, 1841811254

Morningstar, Sally, *The Wiccan Way*, Godsfield Press, 2003, 1841812234

Saxena, Jaya & Zimmerman, Jess, *Basic Witches*, Quirk Books, 2017, 9781594749773

Van de Car, Nikki, *Practical Magic*, Running Press, 2017, 9780762463077